SWEET AND SAD

Conversations on September 11, 2011
The Tenth Anniversary of 9/11

Play 2
The Apple Family
Scenes from Life in the Country

Richard Nelson

BROADWAY PLAY PUBLISHING INC
New York
BroadwayPlayPub.com

First printing: October 2011
Second printing: February 2012
Third printing: October 2012
I S B N: 978-0-88145-518-2

Book design: Marie Donovan
Page make-up: Adobe Indesign
Typeface: Palatino
Printed and bound in the U S A

PLAYS BY RICHARD NELSON

Artists In America:
FRANK'S HOME*
FAREWELL TO THE THEATRE
(scheduled for production)
NIKOLAI AND THE OTHERS
(scheduled for production)

Plays of Adolescence, A Trilogy:
GOODNIGHT CHILDREN EVERYWHERE
FRANNY'S WAY*
MADAME MELVILLE

England/America, A Special Relationship:
SOME AMERICANS ABROAD
TWO SHAKESPEAREAN ACTORS
NEW ENGLAND

American History Plays:
COLUMBUS AND THE DISCOVERY OF JAPAN
THE GENERAL FROM AMERICA
HOW SHAKESPEARE WON THE WEST*
CONVERSATIONS IN TUSCULUM

The Apple Family Plays:
Part One: THAT HOPEY CHANGEY THING*
Part Two: SWEET AND SAD*

Other Plays:
BETWEEN EAST AND WEST*

PRINICIPIA SCRIPTORIAE
ROOTS IN WATER*
RODNEY'S WIFE*
MISHA'S PARTY *(with Alexander Gelman)*
LEFT*

Early Plays:
THE KILLING OF YABLONSKI*
SCOOPING*
CONJURING AN EVENT*
JUNGLE COUP*
THE VIENNA NOTES*
BAL*
THE RETURN OF PINOCCHIO*
RIP VAN WINKLE OR 'THE WORKS'*
AN AMERICAN COMEDY*

Musicals:
UNFINISHED PIECE FOR A PLAYER PIANO
(with Peter Golub)
PARADISE FOUND
(with Ellen Fitzhugh & Jonathan Tunick)
MY LIFE WITH ALBERTINE *(with Ricky Ian Gordon)*
JAMES JOYCE'S THE DEAD *(with Shaun Davey)*
CHESS
(with Tim Rice, Benny Andersson, Björn Ulvaeus)

Translations:
Turgenev: A MONTH IN THE COUNTRY
(with Richard Pevear & Lorissa Volokhonsky)
Ibsen: THE WILD DUCK*, ENEMY OF THE PEOPLE
*(also adaptation)**
Strindberg: MISS JULIE*, THE FATHER*
Molière: DON JUAN*
Goldoni: IL CAMPIELLO*
Pirandello: ENRICO IV*
Erdman: THE SUICIDE*
Brecht: JUNGLE OF CITIES, THE WEDDING

Chekhov: THE SEAGULL*, THE CHERRY ORCHARD*,
THREE SISTERS*, THE WOOD DEMON*
Fo: ACCIDENTAL DEATH OF AN ANARCHIST
Carriere: THE CONTROVERSY AT VALLADOID

Adaptations
TYNAN *(with Colin Chambers)*
from the Diaries of Kenneth Tynan
LOLITA *edited for the stage, from the novel by Nabokov*

*Published by Broadway Play Publishing Inc

SWEET AND SAD was commissioned by The Public Theater (Oskar Eustis, Artistic Director; Joey Parnes, Interim Executive Director). The play opened at the Public Theater on 11 September 2011. The cast and creative contributors were:

RICHARD...Jay O Sanders
BARBARA .... Maryann Plunkett
MARIAN...Laila Robins
JANE .... J Smith-Cameron
BENJAMIN ....Jon DeVries
TIM...Shuler Hensley

Director... Richard Nelson
Set & costume design....................................Susan Hilferty
Lighting design ....Jennifer Tipton
Sound design........................... Scott Lehrer & Will Pickens
Production stage manager ....Pamela Salling
Stage manager... Maggie Swing
Assistant director....................................David F Chapman
Stage management intern........................Jared Oberholtzer

CHARACTERS & SETTING

The APPLES:

RICHARD APPLE, *a lawyer, lives in Manhattan.*

BARBARA APPLE, *his sister, a high school English teacher, lives in Rhinebeck.*

MARIAN APPLE PLATT, *his sister, a second-grade teacher. Lives in Rhinebeck.*

JANE APPLE HALLS, *his sister, a non-fiction writer and teacher, lives with* TIM *in Manhattan.*

BENJAMIN APPLE, *his uncle, a retired actor, lives with* BARBARA *and* MARIAN *in Rhinebeck.*

TIM ANDREWS, *an actor.*

The play takes place between approximately 2 P M and 4 P M on the afternoon of Sunday, September 11, 2011

Rhinebeck, New York; a small historic village one hundred miles north of New York City; once referred to in an article in The New York Times *as "The Town That Time Forgot". A room in* BARBARA APPLE's *house, which she shares with* BENJAMIN *and* MARIAN, *on Center Street.*

"The strong forget."
Herzog, Saul Bellow

for Oskar and the Public Theater

(A wooden table and three wooden chairs. A few short-stemmed flowers in a small glass bowl on the table. Rugs)

(Beirut's Scenic World *begins;* BARBARA *enters with a tablecloth, which she lays over the table; soon* MARIAN *and* BENJAMIN *bring in plates, silverware, glasses, etc. which they set in the middle of the table.* BARBARA *leaves.* MARIAN *goes off in a different direction.)*

(Then RICHARD *enters and sits at the table with Benjamin, both with coffee cups.* MARIAN *returns and joins them at the table. The Beirut fades, and from a C D playing in the next room, we hear Duruflé's* Requiem, The Kyrie*)*

(Lights come up on them listening.)

The Kyrie

(Music plays. Pause)

RICHARD: It's very beautiful.

MARIAN: It is…

(They listen. BENJAMIN *starts to stand.)*

MARIAN: Where are you going?

BENJAMIN: *(Holding out his hand)* Could I have a cigarette?

MARIAN: You just had one. No.

*(*BENJAMIN *gives* MARIAN *a look and sits back down.)*

*(*RICHARD *watches this. Music plays.)*

RICHARD: Listen to the music, Uncle. *(About the music)* How often do they rehearse?

MARIAN: Once a week. At night. Tuesday nights. *(She smiles, listening.)*

RICHARD: What?

MARIAN: The pianist. He never wears shoes. He plays barefoot. Barbara says he's always there.

RICHARD: Why doesn't he wear shoes?

MARIAN: *(She shrugs.)* I don't know. I don't know. Listen to this.

(They listen; MARIAN looks at her brother, reaches out and takes his hand and holds it.)

(Then:)

MARIAN: Barbara says—it's a phenomenal feeling, singing in a group that size.

RICHARD: How big is the—?

MARIAN: Hundred and twenty maybe. Hundred and thirty? And all ages. Not just from the community, but Bard students too. You should come up and hear one of their concerts, they perform in a beautiful new theater. Right on the campus.

RICHARD: Where they do the summer— [festival]?

MARIAN: Same place…

RICHARD: Have you been to one of these concerts, Uncle?

MARIAN: *(As he turns to her, answering for him)* He has.

RICHARD: This is from last Christmas, you said?

MARIAN: Their Christmas concert… *(To Uncle)* You were there. *(Then)* She says she feels like she's part of something. Something big. Or bigger.

RICHARD: I can imagine that.

MARIAN: The conductor's a very nice man. Smart. He makes it fun.

RICHARD: I wish I could sing. So what's stopping you? You should join. Barbara's right.

MARIAN: Maybe.

RICHARD: You sing.

MARIAN: I don't know.

RICHARD: You should get out.

MARIAN: I get out, Richard. *(Points out:)* The altos… *(She looks at him.)*

(Then sound of car doors closing interrupts.)

MARIAN: That's them. That's Barbara's car. I have to turn that off. *(She is up.)*

RICHARD: Why do you have to—?

MARIAN: And—. *(Looks around, then gesturing toward the living room)* Hide in here—.

RICHARD: What? Why—?

MARIAN: Hide. Hide! Come on, Richard. Uncle, shsh. Don't say anything.

RICHARD: *(Getting up)* My car's out front.

MARIAN: You said it was a rent-a-car. Hide! Wait, take your cup. Please. I want to see their faces…

(MARIAN hurries off into the living room. BENJAMIN and RICHARD share a look. BENJAMIN hands him his cup.)

(the music suddenly goes off in the other room. MARIAN hurries back in.)

MARIAN: *(Hurrying through)* Hide! Will you just hide? Get in there!

(MARIAN pushes RICHARD Off into the living room and she hurries off into the kitchen.)

(Greetings off in the kitchen; BENJAMIN *is alone, confused.)*
(Lights fade.)

Richard

(Moments later, BARBARA, MARIAN *and* JANE *enter from the kitchen, talking.* BENJAMIN *sits at the table.)*

JANE: *(Entering)* Sorry we're so late.

MARIAN: That's not your fault—.

BARBARA: *(This explains everything)* Amtrak…

JANE: *(To* MARIAN*)* You look good.

MARIAN: *(To* BARBARA*)* What did she expect, Barbara? *(Makes a funny "sad" face)*

JANE: I meant, I like the blouse. I didn't "expect" anything.

*(*MARIAN *is smiling.)*

BARBARA: *(To* BENJAMIN*)* You know who this is, Benjamin.

JANE: *(To* MARIAN*)* Why are you smiling like that?

BARBARA: Say hi to Benjamin.

JANE: *(To* BENJAMIN*)* It's so good to see you, Uncle. It's been a while, hasn't it? How are you doing? He's looking great. *(To* BENJAMIN. *A joke)* I think the word is "dapper". *(She gives him an awkward kiss on the cheek. To* BARBARA:*)* Is this what he's going to wear for the reading?

BARBARA: He's going to change. He's got a suit.

MARIAN: *(Playfully, messing up* BENJAMIN's *hair)* He's hungry. So he's grumpy.

BENJAMIN: *(To* MARIAN*)* Stop that.

JANE: Are you hungry, Uncle? Tim and I can't wait to see you 'perform.'

BARBARA: *(To* BENJAMIN*)* It's Jane.

BENJAMIN: I know it's Jane.

MARIAN: *(To* BARBARA*)* He doesn't know who she is.

(To BENJAMIN*)* She's our sister, Uncle Benjamin.

BENJAMIN: I know who Jane is. When are we going to eat?

MARIAN: He likes to eat early. Too early, I think. *(To* BENJAMIN*)* They're late. The train was late.

BARBARA: And the reading's—.

JANE: That's at five? We have time. We're not that late.

MARIAN: *(To* BARBARA*)* I kept everything warm in the oven…

JANE: *(To* BENJAMIN*)* We haven't seen you act since— for ages? *(To* BARBARA*)* The last time, was that at the Y?

BARBARA: *(To* BENJAMIN*)* When you did your Oscar Wilde at the Y in New York.

MARIAN: *(Interrupting)* Shsh!

BARBARA: What are you doing?

MARIAN: Both of you, Shsh.

(They are confused.)

BARBARA: We're talking. *(Continuing to* BENJAMIN*)* Jane and Tim have come up to see your reading, Uncle.

MARIAN: Shsh! I have a surprise!

BARBARA: What surprise?

BENJAMIN: And Richard.

JANE: What?

MARIAN: Benjamin—!

BENJAMIN: And Richard's come up. He's here.

(BARBARA *and* JANE *are confused.*)

BARBARA: Richard?

JANE: What do you mean? What are you talking about? Richard's not here.

MARIAN: Uncle—

BENJAMIN: He's here. *(To* MARIAN*)* Isn't he here? *(To* JANE *and* BARBARA*)* He went in there. *(Points, then calls)* Aren't you in there, Richard?

(RICHARD *comes out.*)

(JANE *is stunned.*)

RICHARD: Surprise...

JANE: What is he doing here?

MARIAN: *(To* BENJAMIN*)* Why did you tell them?

JANE: *(To* RICHARD*)* What are you doing?

BARBARA: *(Over this, to* MARIAN*)* When did he get here?

MARIAN: I wanted to surprise you. *(Explaining)* He just walked in. Didn't even knock. I turned around—. I just screamed.

JANE: *(To* RICHARD*)* Why are you here? *(To* BARBARA*)* You said he couldn't come.

BARBARA: He called this morning. I didn't tell them, Richard.

RICHARD: It's good to see you too, Jane.

JANE: I didn't mean—. *(As she hugs him)* I'm just surprised. That's not your car—.

RICHARD: Pamela's taking the kids somewhere...

MARIAN: It's a rental.

BARBARA: *(To* MARIAN*)* He told me not to tell you. All of a sudden, he says he wants to come to the reading.

MARIAN: You knew he—?

BARBARA: I wanted it to be a surprise... *(To* JANE*)* Jane, my turn. *(As she hugs him) I'm* happy to see you.

JANE: So am I.

MARIAN: It was a surprise.

BARBARA: Good! It worked.

JANE: *(To* RICHARD*)* You could have driven us up. We took the train—.

RICHARD: I didn't know—.

BARBARA: *(for him)* He decided at the last minute. He told me this on the phone. He wanted to come...

(Lights fade.)

Tim & Jane

(Lights up a moment later)

JANE: That train was so late, Uncle. You must be starving.

BARBARA: *(To* MARIAN*)* Give him a cigarette. That's what he wants.

MARIAN: *(Giving* BENJAMIN *a cigarette)* Everything's ready. We can eat now—.

*(*JANE *watches* BENJAMIN *take the cigarette.)*

MARIAN: We don't let him smoke in the house.

BARBARA: Marian doesn't...

(They watch BENJAMIN *go off with his cigarette.)*

BARBARA: *(Under her breath)* Not even in a hurricane.

MARIAN: That's not true.

JANE: When did this start?

(After MARIAN *looks to* BARBARA*)*

MARIAN: You didn't know that he's smoking now? *(Shakes her head, then to* BARBARA*)* Why do you always want to keep everything quiet?

BARBARA: I don't always want to keep—

MARIAN: Like it'll go away. We should talk, Jane. About Benjamin. You too, Richard.

JANE: *(To* RICHARD*)* Do you know about this—?

RICHARD: No.

MARIAN: *(Over this)* And you try and say anything to her *(*BARBARA*)* about this and she just goes quiet. See what I mean? There. See what I live with? She always used to do that.

RICHARD: I don't remember Barbara doing that.

MARIAN: Maybe just with me and Jane. A sister thing. Jane remembers.

RICHARD: *(To* JANE*)* Do you—?

*(*JANE *doesn't.)*

BARBARA: I thought we were going to eat.

JANE: Can we fit around the table?

BARBARA: *(Heading off, calls back)* Richard's here… We'll use the card table. We can do a buffet. It'll be more comfortable. If that's all right with everyone…

RICHARD: *(Joking)* I didn't mean to cause a problem.

JANE: *(Joking)* Why stop now?

MARIAN: *(To* BARBARA*)* Are you asking me?

BARBARA: Is that all right, Marian? *(She is gone.)*

MARIAN: Benjamin smokes almost a pack a day now. Barbara says he used to smoke in his twenties. She remembers this… She thinks something just—I don't know. *(Snaps her fingers)* And now he's back in his twenties so he's smoking. *(She heads off. Happily shouts to* BARBARA*)* Barbara, Richard's here!

JANE: *(To "the world")* So am I…

(They are alone.)

RICHARD: He's now smoking. *(To* JANE*)* I can take you back.

JANE: We're staying the night.

RICHARD: Right.

JANE: *(Then)* Tim's with me.

RICHARD: Barbara said that.

JANE: What did she say?

RICHARD: That—Tim would be here.

JANE: We dropped him off in town. He wanted to—buy some wine.

RICHARD: I stopped there too.

JANE: We're together. Again.

RICHARD: I heard that somewhere. We do share two sisters.

JANE: And what do they say? I'm curious.

RICHARD: No one's criticizing you, Jane. I like Tim.

JANE: I'm sorry I haven't called… It's been—crazy.

RICHARD: Have you been up here—recently?

JANE: No. You?

*(*RICHARD *shakes his head.)*

JANE: Marian looks pretty good. She's teaching. I was surprised when I heard she'd moved in. Weren't you?

RICHARD: *(Shrugs)* They shared a room for a while as kids.

JANE: I guess I forgot that.

(BARBARA *enters lugging a card table.*)

BARBARA: *(To* JANE*)* Tim's here.

RICHARD: That's no longer news.

BARBARA: He's in the kitchen.

RICHARD: *(To* BARBARA*)* Can I help with that?

JANE: What can I do?

BARBARA: *(Shrugs)* Bring in things.

JANE: I'm very sorry to hear that Uncle's smoking. *(She starts to go off.)*

BARBARA: *(Setting up the card table)* He got lost this week.

(This stops JANE.*)*

JANE: What? What do you mean?

BARBARA: That really upset Marian. He went off to the C V S—for cigarettes. It's just down the street—.

RICHARD: I know the C V S.

BARBARA: I get a call from one of my students...

*(MARIAN *returns with a tray of bowls—vegetables, potatoes, etc...*)*

BARBARA: She thinks she's seen my Uncle about a mile and half down Route 9. *(Looks at* MARIAN *then)* We drive down and there he is walking, just walking.

MARIAN: *(Setting out the bowls)* I'm glad you're worried too, Barbara.

BARBARA: Of course I'm worried.

MARIAN: *(To* RICHARD *&* JANE*)* He sneaks out to Fosters. He won't admit it—.

BARBARA: Marian—

MARIAN: I have a friend who's a waitress... He sits at the bar.

JANE: What's wrong with that?

MARIAN: Buys people drinks. People he doesn't know.

RICHARD: *(Trying to make a joke)* How does he know he doesn't know them?

MARIAN: They take advantage of him, Richard.

(TIM enters with two bottles of wine, and some glasses; his hands full.)

TIM: Where do you want all this? *(Greeting)* Richard! They just told me—.

RICHARD: Tim! *(To the others)* Tim's here.

JANE: That was quick.

BARBARA: *(To TIM)* On the card table. First, let me put the tablecloth on… *(She flaps open the table cloth.)*

JANE: You bought two bottles.

TIM: You asked me to. Red and white.

MARIAN: We just got Benjamin—finally—drinking the non-alcoholic… *(To RICHARD)* He really doesn't know the difference.

JANE: *(To MARIAN)* I doubt that very much.

TIM: *(Hands full)* Richard, I'll shake hands in a minute—.

MARIAN: *(Over this)* He doesn't, Jane.

JANE: We are celebrating his show, Marian…

BARBARA: *(Under her breath)* That's what I said…

MARIAN: It's not a show. And I certainly wouldn't call it celebrating, Jane. So we should be encouraging him to get drunk? He doesn't need any encouragement for that… *(She goes off into the kitchen.)*

JANE: I'll bring in things. *(She heads off.)*

RICHARD: *(To* TIM*)* I put a bottle in the fridge. *(Then)* It's alcoholic too.

BARBARA: I'll get another tablecloth, this one has a stain.

*(*BARBARA *heads off. The men are alone.* TIM *Still has his hands full.)*

RICHARD: I didn't think I could come—. A last minute thing.

TIM: That's what Barbara just—. A nice surprise. *(Shows* RICHARD *that his hands are still full)*

RICHARD: They could make you hold that all day. I know my sisters. *(Then)* They like being waited on.

TIM: *(Awkward joke)* If that's the worst that can happen to me.

*(*TIM *laughs,* RICHARD *doesn't.)*

RICHARD: What do you think can happen to you? We all like you, Tim. You're welcome here. Let me help you.

TIM: I got it. I'm fine. *(Then)* Rhinebeck hasn't changed. Looks the same.

*(*BARBARA *returns with another tablecloth for the card table.)*

RICHARD: And really nice to be out of the city. Especially today.

TIM: *(With emphasis)* Especially today.

*(*JANE *carries in two chairs.)*

RICHARD: *(To* JANE*)* I could have done that.

JANE: Then why didn't you?

(Off, church bells—playing a hymn.)

TIM: Are those church bells? They're lovely... This is such a charming town. You're lucky to live here, Barbara.

(MARIAN *returns with bowls, etc., etc.*)

RICHARD: *(To* JANE*)* Should I get my bottle?

JANE: What's wrong with Tim's two bottles?

BARBARA: *(Setting up the tablecloth, to* TIM*)* Those aren't real bells by the way.

TIM: What do you mean?

MARIAN: It's the Dutch Reformed—they play C Ds of bell music through loud speakers in their steeple. Barbara hates that.

TIM: *(Innocently)* Why do you—?

BARBARA: We'll set out the salad here too. *(Then back to the bells)* Why should they be allowed to blast us with their C Ds? I mean, if they were bells and real people were ringing them—okay. I get it. But they're just stupid C Ds. At Christmas it's the worst. Like you're living inside a mall. Who the hell do they think they are? I mean, if I stuck a speaker out of my goddamn window and played it whenever I wanted to play it, they'd come and arrest me... *(She goes off.)*

MARIAN: See...

(Short pause as they set out the rest.)

MARIAN: Thank you, Tim.

TIM: *(To shake hands)* Richard, good to see you.

RICHARD: And you. *(To sisters, a bad joke one more time)* Tim's here.

(As BARBARA *and now* BENJAMIN *return with another chair, more bowls, etc.)*

RICHARD: What else can I do?

BARBARA: What "else"? What have you done?

JANE: Getting hungry, Uncle Benjamin?

BARBARA: He likes to eat lunch now at eleven.

MARIAN: And I don't know why you let him do that.

RICHARD: *(To be useful, moving chairs)* Why don't we have Benjamin sit there. Tim, Marian—there. Barbara—

JANE: It's Barbara's house. You're really going to tell her where to sit? Why do you always do that? *(To* TIM*)* Why do men do that?

TIM: *(On the spot)* I don't know.

BARBARA: It's also now Marian's house, Jane.

(Awkward moment)

BARBARA: I mean, she's not a guest. She lives here too.

(They start to serve themselves.)

RICHARD: You remember Tim, don't you, Uncle?

MARIAN: *(To* BENJAMIN*)* He's the actor. You like him. He's from New York.

BENJAMIN: Always a pleasure to see you, son. I used to live in New York. *(To others)* Of course I remember him.

(Others exchange doubtful looks.)

BENJAMIN: *(To* BARBARA*)* Didn't I live in New York?

*(*BARBARA *nods.)*

TIM: It's great to be up here, sir. Out of the city. *(To* RICHARD*)* Especially today.

MARIAN: *(To* JANE*)* I'm so glad you two are back together. I never liked your husband.

(This stops the conversation for a moment.)

MARIAN: What did I say?

JANE: It is nice. It is very nice... For me. *(She smiles at* TIM.*)*

TIM: *(After a prompt)* And me too.

JANE: Richard, how's Pamela?

RICHARD: She's good.

MARIAN: I'm so sorry she couldn't come too. *(To* BARBARA*)* Aren't we?

(No response)

MARIAN: *(To* RICHARD*)* She couldn't come, right? *(To* BARBARA*)* She's always so busy.

RICHARD: She's doing things with the kids. *(Then:)* She told me to say hi from her to my lovely lovely sisters...

(Short pause)

MARIAN: Say hi back.

BENJAMIN: *(As he goes to the card table)* Can I get anyone else a glass of wine?

MARIAN: *(Trying to stop him)* We have your favorite wine in the kitchen, Uncle. Let me get it for you—

BENJAMIN: I want this wine. I'd like a change.

(They continue to serve themselves.)

TIM: *(Serving himself)* Look at this. Turkey. Cole slaw. Is this chicken salad? *(To* BARBARA *and* MARIAN*)* You two have gone all out...

MARIAN: *(To* TIM, *pointing out).* Lima beans and carrots... *(About a casserole)* This is vegetarian, Jane... Or are you over with that?

JANE: I'm not "over with that".

BARBARA: *(Suddenly worried)* We didn't rush the dinner, did we? *(Explaining)* The reading's at five... *(Looks at her watch)* And you heat things for too long...

TIM: *(After a look at* JANE*)* No, no...I'm ready to eat.

MARIAN: And Benjamin was getting very hungry.

(They look at BENJAMIN.*)*

BARBARA: I didn't mean to rush us...

JANE: You didn't, Barbara. We were late. *(Then)* After the reading maybe we can take a walk around the village a little. I'd enjoy that. And we are staying the night.

(They serve themselves.)

JANE: Tim couldn't wait to come up here. He loves this village.

RICHARD: You're not thinking of getting a weekend place up here, are you?

JANE: Where would we get that kind of money, Richard? We're not all expensive lawyers.

BARBARA: You don't strike me as the weekender type, any way.

TIM: *(To* BARBARA*)* What is the "weekender type"?

MARIAN: Don't get Barbara started...

(They serve.)

MARIAN: *(To* BARBARA*)* Sunday night, the weekender's are pretty much gone by then. So it'll be nice. *(To* JANE*)* For your walk. *(Then)* A lot of city people were up this weekend.

(Short pause, they serve.)

BARBARA: I hate it when the moment you walk into a house—they serve the meal.

JANE: Barbara, it's fine. What else could we do?

RICHARD: *(To say something)* How late was your train?

TIM: I'll have a roll...

JANE: *(Looks to* TIM*)* Forty, fifty minutes—?

BARBARA: *(To* TIM*)* When Marian first moved to
Rhinebeck? She was the first.

TIM: I know.

BARBARA: She was waiting on the platform at Rhinecliff
and the guy from the ticket office was there; and she
asked him for the time? *(To* MARIAN*)* What did he say?

JANE: *(To* TIM*)* I've heard this—.

RICHARD: *(To* TIM*)* I'd heard it too…

MARIAN: They've heard this.

BARBARA: Tim hasn't. He said, "Honey", he called
Marian honey, Tim. "Honey, I threw away my watch
the day I joined Amtrak."

*(*TIM *laughs.)*

JANE: *(To* TIM*)* I'd told you that story…

(And they have all taken seats and are about to eat, when:)

(Lights fade.)

Up the Hudson

(Lights up a moment later, as they eat:)

TIM: *(Eating)* I love the train.

JANE: *(Surprised)* It's expensive.

MARIAN: Everything goes up.

BARBARA: And Sunday's the worst. It can be cheaper
other days.

TIM: I think that's one of the most beautiful train rides
in America.

BARBARA: *(To* TIM*)* You should ride that train with
Richard sometime—he's the expert.

RICHARD: What are you— [talking about]?

BARBARA: He's like a tour guide—.

MARIAN: *(Over this, adding her two cents to* TIM*)* Like a docent.

BARBARA: Look there. Look at that. Where they tied a chain across the Hudson to stop the British.

MARIAN: In the Revolutionary War.

BARBARA: Bannerman's Castle. West Point.

RICHARD: Jane knows all that too.

BARBARA: Not like you do.

JANE: *(To* RICHARD*)* I've read one book. I told you about one book—.

BARBARA: Or like Richard used to. *(To* TIM*)* Richard used to love that river.

RICHARD: *(Eating)* I still do.

BARBARA: Good. He used to go back and forth to Albany a lot when he worked for the Attorney General's office. Or have you forgotten that?

MARIAN: *(She knows the answer)* Now you don't go back and forth?

RICHARD: No.

MARIAN: I suppose now you just have to walk to Wall Street to meet with your rich clients.

(Looks at BARBARA *and smiles: that made the point.)*

RICHARD: I do *pro bono* work as well. I can live with myself.

(They eat.)

RICHARD: I gather from Marian, she's thinking of joining your community chorus, Barbara.

BARBARA: *(Surprised)* When did she tell you that—?

MARIAN: I'm thinking of it. You've wanted me to think about it.

TIM: *(To* JANE*)* What?

JANE: Barbara's in a chorus at Bard. Marian, are you thinking of joining?

BARBARA: I've been trying to get her—.

RICHARD: *(Over this)* She was playing a C D of your Christmas concert. When I arrived—.

MARIAN: *(Trying to make it a joke)* Snuck in on me.

BARBARA: *(Very interested)* She was? You were?

JANE: *(To* MARIAN*)* Why don't you? You have a good voice. Sounds like fun, doesn't it? You should get out.

MARIAN: I get out.

RICHARD: I said the same thing.

BARBARA: I've tried to get you to listen to that C D a hundred times.

JANE: I think it's a great idea.

MARIAN: I get out. School's started. I teach every day. I went to church this morning.

BARBARA: She's getting out now.

(They eat.)

TIM: *(To* MARIAN*)* How was today's service in church? Do they do anything special up here today?

BARBARA: There's our concert tonight—.

TIM: I meant in church. And did anyone watch any of it on TV this morning? I thought the garden they made looked quite beautiful… Those rows and rows of trees. Serene and peaceful. That is, once all this noise dies down.

JANE: I thought so too.

RICHARD: They're making it so only a certain number of people at a time can…

JANE: You book on line.

BARBARA: Makes sense. *(Answering the earlier question)* Benjamin and I went with Marian to church…

MARIAN: What she's trying to hint at is—I made them go with me. Which is not true. I can go by myself. I go lots of places by myself. *(To* BARBARA*)* I've seen Adam. I'm not hiding from him.

(They eat.)

MARIAN: I'm not.

BARBARA: *(Continuing to* TIM*)* And they did something very special in church today, Tim. It was really very nice, wasn't it, Uncle? Very simple.

BENJAMIN: What? I don't know.

BARBARA: You liked it. All the names? *(To the others)* If someone had lost—someone, a friend, a friend's friend, certainly a family member, a loved one—in the towers or I suppose one of the planes … You could have their name read out. It was a pretty long list. I was surprised. *(To* MARIAN*)* Weren't you surprised? All the way up here.

(They eat.)

JANE: So—was Adam there?

MARIAN: Is this all going to be about me?

JANE: Was he there? I'm just asking. Barbara?

*(*MARIAN *nods.* JANE *looks to* RICHARD*.)*

RICHARD: *(To* JANE*)* I've written him twice. I've tried calling him. Marian knows this.

MARIAN: I'm right here.

RICHARD: He should pay something. And it shouldn't be up to Marian to make him.

BARBARA: Talk to Marian.

MARIAN: I know what he's—

RICHARD: Barbara's told me, Marian, you're still paying half of the mortgage. You know, that makes no sense. You're not being— "independent" you're being silly. And I'm not saying you have to fight him. Just that it should be fair...

MARIAN: *(To* JANE*)* I don't want Richard doing anything. He knows this. Can you tell him that?

JANE: He's a lawyer. He's your brother.

MARIAN: And what do *you* get, Jane?

JANE: That's different.

MARIAN: Why is it different? Why is she different?

BARBARA: I'm sorry, Tim.

TIM: No, no, it's...

JANE: *(To* MARIAN*)* Alfred paid for Billy's school. That's all I cared about. That's all I've asked for. And that was a lot. *(Then)* We just want to help you... *(Short pause. She eats.)*

MARIAN: Where is Billy now?

JANE: *(Eating)* Philadelphia. They say, that's a good place for young people. Stay out of New York. It's too unreal now. Too rich. Too many kids with trust funds. *(Eats)* I have a friend who works in Chelsea, in a gallery there, and the kids , the girls—the receptionists—the clothes they wear. Well, I couldn't afford them. None of us could.

BARBARA: Maybe Richard.

JANE: *(Smiles)* Maybe him.

RICHARD: I'm saving for two college educations!

JANE: *(As she eats)* Where do they get the money? It must seem unreal. Especially to impressionable kids. *(Turns to* TIM*)* Tim says it's maybe the one good thing that's come out of the recession.

RICHARD: What is, Tim?

JANE: To be reminded that rich people aren't heroes, just because they're rich. For years now that's been hard to explain to kids. To my son. *(Smiles to herself)*

RICHARD: *("Under his breath" to* TIM*, a joke)* She speaks for you now?

JANE: Rich people just look so appealing—. But then for at least a minute, *(To* TIM*)* right?

RICHARD: *(Teasing to Tim, under his breath)* Say "right".

BARBARA: Richard—

TIM: *(To* JANE*)* Right.

*(*RICHARD *laughs.)*

JANE: Our kids got a chance to take a real good close look at some of those people. And see for themselves—is that what they want to become. *(Then)* But then again, all that's maybe already passed. That's depressing. Uncle you're not the only person around with amnesia. It's disgusting. *(Eats)* And they're getting away with it.

(Pause)

MARIAN: So Alfred paid for Billy's school. Good. And I'm glad Billy is doing so well.

JANE: I didn't say—. He doesn't have a job—.

MARIAN: *(To* RICHARD*)* And how are your children, Richard?

(Others realize the weight behind this.)

RICHARD: They're—fine, Marian.

MARIAN: Good. I'm glad. That's so nice to hear. *(Standing)* Excuse me. I think we need more—*(Looks around)* potatoes...

(MARIAN takes a bowl and goes into the kitchen. The moment she is gone:)

RICHARD: Jane—.

JANE: I'm sorry I didn't mean to start talking about Billy. I'm sorry. I'm sorry. I wasn't thinking. Where is my head?

BARBARA: You can't just stop talking about your kids.

JANE: You said she's getting out of the house now. And she's teaching... That's all good, isn't it?

RICHARD: I could try and see if I can talk some sense into Adam this afternoon. Just go knock on his door.

(BARBARA shakes her head.)

RICHARD: What if he's at the reading? Should I just say nothing? He is getting away with—.

JANE: *(To RICHARD)* What a son of a bitch.

RICHARD: I agree.

JANE: *(To "TIM")* And now Barbara is living in her own basement.

BARBARA: My choice, Jane. There's a bathroom down there.

RICHARD: *(To BARBARA)* And for how long?

BARBARA: For as long as she wants. As long as it takes. It takes time... Give her time—.

JANE: We were brought up to be women who stood up for ourselves—.

(BARBARA sees MARIAN returning with the potatoes and stops the conversation. Short pause)

MARIAN: Richard I thought today was the day every year you always spent with your old buddies. It was a "thing" you did.

BARBARA: More than a "thing", Marian.

MARIAN: I didn't mean—.

RICHARD: I do. I did. We had our breakfast. Same place. Same toasts. Same "buddies". *(Then)* But we—. It felt different today. From other anniversaries. And it was getting very crowded down there. And loud… Anyway, we just stayed a little while. Hence—I could come here. *(Raises his glass to them)*

(BENJAMIN gets up.)

BARBARA: Are you done?

BENJAMIN: No. *(He looks off.)*

MARIAN: Your cigarettes aren't in your room.

BARBARA: Remember, Marian is keeping them for you. Marian, he can have another cigarette.

MARIAN: *(As she doles out a cigarette)* And make sure you use the ashtray.

(BENJAMIN starts to go to the kitchen.)

BENJAMIN: I use the ashtray.

(They watch him go.)

MARIAN: *(Calling after him)* Sometimes you just flick them…

(They eat.)

BARBARA: The mornings are his best time. The best for me too. He's funny. He helps us out in the kitchen, doesn't he? It's when we have our conversations. Our talks. As the day wears on, he gets more and more… quiet. *(Then)* You wonder: Is he watching us? Judging us? That's what Marian—

MARIAN: I do not.

BARBARA: Sometimes. Or just listening? Or is he somewhere else?

MARIAN: *(About* BENJAMIN*)* Shouldn't he have a sweater?

BARBARA: He's fine. *(Then, to* RICHARD*)* So it was just too crowded for you?

RICHARD: Downtown?

JANE: We met a couple on the train—they were escaping the city too, like you, Richard.

RICHARD: I wasn't— "escaping".

JANE: You could see it in their faces. They didn't have to say anything. *(She eats, then:)* It was a beautiful ride up. It's a beautiful river. Tim brought along a kind of guidebook and was reading me things on the train.

*(*MARIAN *gets up and pours heself a glass of wine.)*

BARBARA: About the Hudson?

RICHARD: Taking my job, are you?

TIM: I wasn't—.

RICHARD: I'm joking.

JANE: Like all of American history has flowed down that river…

MARIAN: A lot. Not everything. Don't exaggerate.

TIM: Pretty much.

BARBARA: *(Taking* MARIAN's *side, giving examples of history the Hudson wasn't connected to)* Slavery—the Civil War. *(To* MARIAN*)* I agree with you.

RICHARD: He's praising your river.

MARIAN: Praising or sentimentalizing?

TIM: Actually—the underground railroad, right up the Hudson—.

MARIAN: The gold rush then.

RICHARD: The Mills Mansion. Mister Mills made all that money selling picks and shovels in the gold—

TIM: Not everything. But...

RICHARD: It is a neat river.

(Pause. They eat.)

JANE: How late is the Roosevelt Home open on a Sunday? It is open today? Tim hasn't been.

RICHARD: *(To* TIM*)* You haven't been?

JANE: Today's not a holiday?

RICHARD: The wine store was open.

JANE: He's wanted to see it.

MARIAN: We have the reading. It's not open that late.

JANE: *(To* TIM*)* Tomorrow then. When does it open?

RICHARD: *(Eating)* You walk into that museum, and, Tim—you can walk right into the part that starts with his first term. And—I swear, you will be moved. Amazed. They did this, and this and this *(Snapping his fingers)* Changed the whole damn country. Sort of gives you hope. That things can change. "Hope and change." Where have I heard that before?

BARBARA: Richard—

RICHARD: That's— if there's the will. If it's not all just about "splitting the difference" and— getting re-elected...

BARBARA: Richard. Is this really the day to talk politics?

(Short pause)

RICHARD: I'm not going to say any more, Barbara...

(They eat.)

RICHARD: We were talking about the Hudson... *(Then)* I just read an interesting book. A lot of it's set on the Hudson. About General Lafayette's return to America.

JANE: When was that?

RICHARD: Years after—as an old man. 1820s. The book's by his secretary. It's his secretary's journal. Congress one day up and decides to invite Lafayette back. As a national celebration, I suppose. They felt they needed one at the time, I guess. To remember! *(Smiles)* So he returns. He's broke now.

TIM: I didn't know that.

RICHARD: He'd been nearly guillotined in his own country. *(Then)* The highlight of this trip—is a boat ride up the Hudson.

TIM: How far up?

RICHARD: Albany. *(Eats)* And everywhere along the shore, every town, every hamlet, wants to celebrate him. Thousands and thousands line the riverbanks. Eighty-year-old men—those who had fought alongside the young Lafayette, and who had risked everything to create this country—they pile into boats in their old uniforms, row out to the General to pay their respects. Fireworks light the sky, bands can be heard from the shore.

(BENJAMIN returns in the middle of this, and heads back the table.)

RICHARD: Reading this book, lying in my bed one night, I found myself—imagining the scene. The General and his old pals—sit around on that boat, and after a few drinks, he asks his old comrades in arms: so how has democracy grown in the years I've been away? Are your politicians serving the people?

BARBARA: Richard.

RICHARD: *(Over this)* Is business fair? Elections, are they honest?

BARBARA: Richard…

BENJAMIN: *(Confused, to* RICHARD*)* What—?

BARBARA: Nothing, Uncle. Nothing.

RICHARD: The same old thing, Uncle. "Hope and Change." Let's talk about something else.

(Lights fade.)

Ghosts

(A short time later, lights up. As they eat, TIM *has just begun a story.)*

TIM: First you walk up these, this stairway—nothing's been changed, touched for fifty, sixty years.

BARBARA: Like what?

TIM: The names on the doors. On the bubbly glass. Old little firms. An accountant. Someone else—casting agent I think. The stenciled names are still there. Anyway, we get to the top of the theater—to Mister Belasco's apartment.

BARBARA: *(To* BENJAMIN*)* I didn't know they lived in their theaters.

BENJAMIN: Oh yes.

RICHARD: *(To* BENJAMIN*)* You remember that?

JANE: *(To* BARBARA*)* Some did. Many did. They had fancy apartments. Tell them about the apartment.

TIM: Most of it's been—stripped; god knows where it's all gone. But there's a safe. A locked safe. Just sitting in the first room we go into. Then... Well the ceiling is quite low. Belasco was a very short man.

(JANE *smiles at the others; they are interested.*)

JANE: *(Prompting* TIM*)* The collar.

BARBARA: What?

TIM: He used to turn his collar around and so he looked like a priest.

BARBARA: That's weird.

MARIAN: Why would he do that?

RICHARD: *(To* TIM*)* You were doing a play in this theater.

TIM: *(nods)* It's all changed now. It's all been renovated.

JANE: He was called "The Bishop of Broadway".

BARBARA: That's creepy.

JANE: It gets worse. Or something. *(Prompting)* The bedroom...

TIM: There's a big wooden structure. Carved dark mahogany I think. Very gothic. In this—the bedroom. It looks like a confessional you'd find in a Catholic church. But larger. Then our stage manager, he'd been given a tour himself. Now he's showing us. He shows us a door to a very small elevator—which goes down to the stage. And a little window—you can look down on the stage through this window from this bedroom. And so he'd—Mister Belasco—he'd phone down to *his* stage manager, having chosen a girl out of the chorus; she'd then be put in the tiny elevator up to his apartment—and the first thing she'd see was this large confessional—which, well, it was large enough for a small bed.

RICHARD: Christ...

JANE: He'd obviously, like a priest, open the little shuttered window, look through at the girl in the bed…

BARBARA: Wow. *(To* BENJAMIN*)* Is that how theater was in your day, Uncle?

BENJAMIN: I hope so.

(They laugh.)

JANE: Did you ever do a play at the Belasco?

BENJAMIN: I don't remember.

*(*JANE *looks to* BARBARA*.)*

BARBARA: I don't know.

TIM: Anyway, that's a very long story just to explain… *(Now the story he wants to tell)* We're in tech. Late one night. The director calls it quits for the day. We all go. Then I'm at Joe's and I realize I've left my sweater—my cashmere sweater—back in the theater. The stage door guy lets me in. The theater's dark, just the ghost light's on. I feel my way along the seats—I remembered leaving it in the back. That's when I heard… *(Pause for effect)*

MARIAN: What?

TIM: The elevator. The little elevator. Which we'd been told couldn't work anymore. Hadn't worked for years. Just this… *(He makes the sound.)*

MARIAN: You're sure it was—.

TIM: That's what I told myself. Must be a dimmer or something… Something left on. 'Hello?' I say. Nothing. I keep working my way through a row of seats, trying not to bang my shin—when I look up and there is a dim light coming from the stage left box. *(Then)* There's a woman there. She's crying. She has a scarf, which covers a lot of her face.

MARIAN: You could hear her…?

TIM: Yes. I could hear her. I find my sweater. It'd fallen between two seats, and lean over—and as I lean I feel a hand on my shoulder.

(MARIAN *reacts*.)

RICHARD: *(To* MARIAN*)* Are you all right?

TIM: *(Continuing)* I swear to god. That's what I feel. There is no one there. But I felt it. Felt someone's fingers… *(Then)* She wasn't in the box anymore.

JANE: And then he hurried like hell out into 44th Street.

(Others relax.)

RICHARD: I'll bet you did. *(Laughs)*

JANE: Supposedly, one of these chorus girls— something had happened in that bedroom and she'd died. In his apartment. *(To* TIM*)* Five, six other people?

*(*TIM *nods.)*

JANE: Have seen her too. He learned this. Once he told some friends about it, and they'd heard the same story. She's always crying.

TIM: *(Teasing* BARBARA*)* I can still feel her fingers…

JANE: *(Ignoring him)* Now that they've renovated…

RICHARD: So she's moved on?

JANE: *(Laughs)* Probably.

TIM: Or went to L A for pilot season and never came back.

(He, JANE *and* BENJAMIN *laugh.)*

MARIAN: I didn't understand…

TIM: I'm sorry. How did I get talking about—?

JANE: I don't know.

RICHARD: Barbara—.

BARBARA: I was telling Tim about the show Benjamin and I saw. It was at the Belasco.

RICHARD: That's right. I remember.

BARBARA: Richard, you got us the tickets. What was the show? *(To* BENJAMIN*)* You liked it.

BENJAMIN: Did I? You're always telling me what I've liked and didn't like. What I've done. *(To others)* It's a very curious relationship to have with another person.

RICHARD: Is it. Not for me. I have Pamela.

(The sisters like this, laugh.)

BARBARA: You shouldn't talk like that about your wife.

RICHARD: It was a joke.

BARBARA: You shouldn't joke…

RICHARD: Then why are you laughing?

BENJAMIN: *(To* TIM*)* Tim?

(This gets their attention.)

BENJAMIN: Tim??

(Others nod.)

BENJAMIN: Are you in a play now? You're an actor?

BARBARA: He is an actor too, Uncle. Like you.

MARIAN: I think Tim told us he did mostly T V.

TIM: Actually, I'm… What? *(Turns to* JANE*)*

MARIAN: You don't know? You have to ask her?

BARBARA: *(To* RICHARD*)* She's worse than Pamela.

(Laughter, except for RICHARD*)*

JANE: Be quiet. Tim's got himself a—.

TIM: Jane, they don't want—.

JANE: A very good gig now—at a restaurant.

RICHARD: At a restaurant? What do you mean?

JANE: Right below where we live now at Manhattan Plaza. *(To* TIM*)* Can I tell them?

(TIM *nods.*)

JANE: Really nice people. A lot of other terrific actors… So when one of them gets an acting job, they let you out. And then… They take you back.

RICHARD: That sounds convenient.

TIM: It is.

JANE: Tim does a lot of readings too.

TIM: They pay like shit. Excuse my French. But they keep you—limber.

MARIAN: Limber? Don't you sit in a reading?

JANE: Actually, maybe you all could help us figure something out.

TIM: Jane—.

BARBARA: Figure out what?

JANE: Maybe it'll help to talk about it.

BARBARA: About what?

JANE: Tim's been offered—. *(To* TIM*)* You want to tell them?

TIM: You can tell them.

JANE: *(Then)* Another restaurant/bar has been trying to poach him. *(She smiles at* TIM*.)* He's that good a waiter. More hours. A set schedule. He's not sure whether he should take it.

TIM: I'm an actor.

JANE: It's a very tough… The economy… The theater especially… You can imagine. You have to be employed—his union says—a certain number of weeks to get the health insurance. He hasn't worked that many weeks. This bar they have some benefits.

RICHARD: If it's the high deductible crap—that's worthless. Do you know?

TIM: I don't know. I don't know anything about health insurance.

BARBARA: You should know—.

JANE: *(To* TIM*)* You haven't asked—.

RICHARD: You need to find out. You need to know what questions to ask.

TIM: I don't think I'm going to take it. So... *(Looks at* JANE*)*

JANE: That's not what you said this... *(To others)* We go back and forth. He's a wonderful actor. I can't take my eyes off of him when he's on stage. Can I? *(She kisses him on the cheek, then:)*

(They eat. Short pause)

BARBARA: How's your book, Jane? You haven't said a word about that.

BENJAMIN: What—?

RICHARD: Jane's magnum opus on American manners...

JANE: Don't make fun.

RICHARD: I wasn't making fun. It sounds like a brilliant book. I'm waiting to read it.

JANE: It's almost done. It's with an editor. They're thinking about it.

TIM: *(Trying to help)* She sent it to her son to read. She's dedicating it to Billy.

MARIAN: Are you? That must make him...

JANE: He hasn't read it yet. He's busy. *(To herself)* Children...

TIM: *(Trying to help)* Jane's trying to sell one chapter as an essay to Playbill.

BARBARA: *(To* RICHARD, *explaining)* That's the little magazine they give you free—.

RICHARD: I know. I have gone to the theater. When I can't avoid it.

TIM: An article about audiences. How things haven't changed. It's very funny.

BARBARA: Why is it funny?…

TIM: Tell them about the German conductor.

JANE: They don't want to hear—.

BARBARA: What German conductor?

TIM: He's giving an outdoor concert in New York in something like—1850? And as soon as he starts, people start talking. One guy makes a lot of noise lighting up his cigar. So—what does the conductor do? He stops the orchestra, looks out into the audience and says to the man— *(Turns to* JANE*)*

JANE: "Go on, sir, don't mind us." It's not that funny.

BARBARA: Just like with cell phones today.

JANE: That is my point.

TIM: What's changed?

JANE: People have been rude for—forever.

RICHARD: I think it's gotten worse. Do you ever go to the movies?

TIM: She has a lot of little stories like that. About audiences.

JANE: Tim told me one. It's in the article.

TIM: I heard an older actor tell it. Whether it happened or—

BARBARA: What?

(TIM *looks to* JANE.)

JANE: It's your story.

TIM: *(Then)* A very established actor—like yourself, Benjamin. He takes another much younger actor under his wing. And he's explaining about audiences to this young man. He says, son.

RICHARD: What's his name? The older actor. Is he famous?

JANE: It doesn't matter.

BARBARA: Pass around the turkey. *(To* MARIAN*)* We bought too much. There's plenty of turkey.

MARIAN: I told you—.

JANE: Tim's trying to—. I thought you wanted to hear this.

(They quiet down.)

BENJAMIN: Was I famous?

MARIAN: *(After a look around the table)* To all of us, Uncle.

JANE: Tim…

TIM: *(Continuing)* Son, the Older Actor says, pretend for a second you're in say— London during the Blitz. And the Germans are attacking, women and children are dying, the city's on fire. And you walk into a theater—

RICHARD: The theaters were open during the Blitz?

JANE: Yes, they were.

TIM: *(Continues)* And you hear an actor give this speech, this way: *(He stands.)* "Once more unto the breach, dear friends, once more; Or close the wall up with our English dead!"

BENJAMIN: I know that.

BARBARA: Where's it from?

(They wait, he doesn't answer, then)

TIM: *(Continuing)* The older actor asks the younger one, how would that make you feel, hearing that? And the young man says, "it would make me feel like I'd want to fight, and beat those Nazis!"

(Food is being passed around.)

BARBARA: *(Explaining)* The young man's an actor too.

JANE: He said that.

MARIAN: Is he?

TIM: The older then says—now let's pretend we are in say, America during another war—the Vietnam War. And people are protesting, and you know innocent women and children are dying over there. And you walk into a theater—.

BARBARA: There was theater then, Richard.

RICHARD: I know, I remember.

TIM: *(Continues)* And hear the same actor— *(A joke to* JANE*)* he must be on tour—

*(*JANE *laughs.)*

TIM: —give the same speech, the same way:
"Once more unto the breach, dear friends, once more;
Or—

BENJAMIN: "—or close the wall up with our English dead!"

BARBARA: He remembers.

JANE: Tim just said it.

BARBARA: Still he remembered that.

RICHARD: Good for you, Uncle.

TIM: *(Continuing)* And now—how does *that* make you feel, the older actor asks. And the young man says— that sounds just loud, and thoughtless.

(For the first time during this story, everyone is paying full attention.)

TIM: The same words. The same actor. The same way.
—What is different? *(He looks around at the others.)*
What's different?

BENJAMIN: The audience.

(The others are amazed and pleased.)

JANE: *(nodding)* The audience. What we, the audience, bring when we come to theater— What we might be feeling that day. What might have happened to us. That is a big part of what a play is.

(They continue to eat and dish out seconds.)

RICHARD: It that really true?

JANE: We may think we're just sitting back, watching— but in a way we're as much a part of what is happening in that theater, as any actor on the stage…

(They eat.)

TIM: *(Serving himself)* I did a show in Boston around 9/11? There was a song, a joyous, funny song in the show, called *Wake The Dead*. On September 10th, the audience cheered and laughed. On September 12th, they wept. Same song…

(Lights fade.)

More Ghosts

(Lights up a moment later.)

JANE: We're also writing a screenplay together.

BARBARA: About—?

JANE: We keep changing our idea. But it'll be something for Tim to act in.

(JANE *looks to* TIM *who nods.*)

MARIAN: *(Trying to be 'funny')* I think you should write a movie about a lawyer who leaves his job helping ordinary people, and goes to work for the rich. And starts watching FOX. And hating teachers... *(Smiles)*

RICHARD: You know me better than that. Don't put me in a box.

(Short pause)

BARBARA: The reason I brought up going to the theater—

MARIAN: *(Interrupts, to* TIM*)* I believe in ghosts. I believe that girl or woman was there. And she touched you.

BARBARA: Marian...

TIM: It felt real.

MARIAN: I've seen a ghost. I've heard her. I've talked to her. I've felt her hand on my shoulder.

(This has stopped the room.)

BARBARA: Are you talking about Evan?

(Others don't know what to do.)

MARIAN: I know—I know it's in my head. But who says ghosts can't be in our head? I call her cell phone. Two, three times a week, don't I?

(MARIAN looks to BARBARA who is about to say something:)

MARIAN: Sometimes more.

RICHARD: *(To BARBARA)* I didn't know that.

MARIAN: Adam still pays for her phone. Maybe because he calls her too? *(Smiles)* So I call, to hear her message. I hear my daughter's voice. I talk. And more often than not, I think she hears me...

JANE: I'm sure she does, Marian.

MARIAN: Don't patronize me.

(Short pause. No one knows what to say.)

MARIAN: *(To* TIM, *as if the most natural thing in the world)* I only say this because we were talking about ghosts…

TIM: I'm sorry if I—.

MARIAN: You didn't do anything.

(Short pause)

BARBARA: *(Pushing forward)* As I was saying, the reason I brought up going to the theater with Benjamin— which led to—the ghost in the theater, very interesting story, Tim. Well, it's because Marian and I—.

MARIAN: What?

BARBARA: Uncle Benjamin. What we've been doing with you.

MARIAN: You, not me. You're the one doing this.

BENJAMIN: Doing what?

RICHARD: *(To* BENJAMIN*)* Don't you know?

BARBARA: *(To* MARIAN*)* You're helping. We're doing this together.

JANE: What?

BARBARA: We've been asking Benjamin questions— mostly about his life, and his career as an actor—and recording them.

MARIAN: She asks him questions—.

BARBARA: *(Over this)* And Marian transcribes them.

MARIAN: You do most of that too.

BARBARA: Not true. We do it together.

JANE: Are you thinking of writing a book?

BARBARA: We're just asking questions. We'll get the notes if you'd like. And show you. You might be interested. Marian, maybe you could get it?

MARIAN: You're asking? *(Stands up)* She never asks you to do anything. *(To* BARBARA*)* You know how hard that is to live with? *(As she goes)* I'm kidding.

BARBARA: It's on the desk. *(Calls)* And bring the tape recorder! There's a tape in it. *(To the others)* I was transcribing earlier...

(As soon as MARIAN *is gone)*

TIM: I haven't known what to say about her daughter. So I haven't said anything. I am so sorry.

RICHARD: That's probably best, Tim.

JANE: I don't know.

TIM: Jane and I weren't together when she died.

JANE: They know that. You sent a lovely note. He read it to me.

BARBARA: And Marian appreciated the gesture. *(Making a joke)* At first she didn't know "who the hell Tim was?" Then I told her and she appreciated it.

BENJAMIN: What are you talking about?

BARBARA: Evan, Uncle. Marian's daughter, Evan...

*(*MARIAN *returns with a large notebook and a small tape recorder.)*

JANE: So—what sort of questions?

BARBARA: You'll see. *(Taking the notebook)* Thanks.

RICHARD: You going to play that—?

BARBARA: It's hard to hear. Most of the time I have to hold that up to my head. *(Opens the notebook)* This is the part you wanted them to hear, Uncle.

BENJAMIN: Did I?

BARBARA: Tim, will you read Benjamin? You're an actor.

(BARBARA *hands a copy of the transcript to* TIM, *she keeps a second copy to read from. Reads*) Question: "Why is it important to you to be an actor."

TIM: *(To* JANE*)* I'm interested in this.

BENJAMIN: Me too.

TIM: *(Reads)* Benjamin answers: "Well, it's the most absorbing—" Do you want to read it yourself, Benjamin?

BARBARA: Why don't you do that?

TIM: Come here, sit down. Sit here. Come on.

(BENJAMIN *sits and is given the transcript.*)

TIM: *(Points out in the transcript)* "Benjamin." There.

BARBARA: We want you to read yourself. *(To others)* We'll let him play himself. *(To* MARIAN*)* We haven't done it this way.

MARIAN: No.

BARBARA: *(To* BENJAMIN*)* Go ahead. There. Where I'm pointing. Question: 'Why is it important to you to be an actor.' And you answer:

JANE: Go on, Uncle.

BENJAMIN: *(Reads)* "It's the most absorbing, thoroughly absorbing work that I could do. That I can do. I have at times thought of other things that I could do, and have done; I've thought about many things, from— including being a doctor—but I never took any medical education."

(RICHARD *laughs.*)

BARBARA: He's obviously bullshitting. Aren't you, Uncle?

BENJAMIN: Am I?

BARBARA: I think you are.

RICHARD: I agree.

(BENJAMIN looks up at them.)

BARBARA: Keep reading.

BENJAMIN: *(Reads)* "I've thought of running for election. For Congress. I don't think there is any possibility in which I should likely be elected."

(Others laugh.)

JANE: I'd vote for you, Uncle!

BENJAMIN: *(Reads)* "Most politicians seem to have amnesia but won't admit it. They don't remember any of the promises they've made." *(He laughs. To others)* That's very funny. I like that. He's funny.

JANE: You know he is you, Uncle?

(Laughter)

RICHARD: You'd fit right in.

BARBARA: *(Reads)* "So you would be the honest politician?

BENJAMIN: Yes. Yes.

BARBARA: *(Points)* That was a question. I'm reading. Here.

BENJAMIN: *(Reads)* "I don't say it's a pressing ambition. I'm not going to address it, unless someone comes and offers me the chance, then I'd probably take it. I would love to be a member of Congress…"

BARBARA: *(Reads)* Me. "Uncle, you were telling me why you are an actor." This is interesting. *(Reads)* "What do you bring to a role that is particular to you?"

TIM: Good question.

BENJAMIN: *(Reads)* "I suppose I bring my history, my childhood, upbringing, and maturity, and strangely enough, perhaps I've reached a point in my life where I bring a total confidence—I don't mean a total confidence in the way I play—but in my necessity."

RICHARD: What does he mean?

MARIAN: What do you mean by that, Uncle? Do you remember?

BENJAMIN: I think…

(They wait for him to answer, then)

BARBARA: Me. *(Reads)* "Would you bring the history of your illness—that's part of you now. And your amnesia, that is you, would you bring that into a role, do you think?" *(Helping him)* We turn the page.

BENJAMIN: *(Reads, very interested in this himself)* "I think I would. And I think I would with great satisfaction, pride—bring that history and show how I have survived it. And have actually learned from it. And help others to learn from it."

JANE: *(To BARBARA)* Is he bullshitting?

BENJAMIN: *(Answering)* No, I don't think he is.

RICHARD: Are you sure?

BENJAMIN: It sounds to me like he isn't. I believe him.

BARBARA: Question. *(Reads)* "What have you learned from it?"

BENJAMIN: *(Reads)* "I think I've learned from it the—the limitless capacity of myself, and therefore, I would say of a human being, to recover, to overcome—not to be scathed, robbed of…"

BARBARA: He doesn't finish the thought.

BENJAMIN: *(Reads)* "I do actually believe, I don't know if this is true—all illnesses can be recovered from, except of course death. Which of course isn't an illness..."

JANE: He's not bullshitting...

BARBARA: *(To the others)* We record in the mornings. He's at his best. I told you that.

BENJAMIN: Could I have my wine?

(BARBARA *gives him more his wine.*)

MARIAN: Is this bothering you, Uncle? We can stop.

BENJAMIN: No. No.

BARBARA: Me. *(Reads)* "When you're doing your Oscar Wilde performance that we've seen you do in New York this past—the reading you did at the Y. Are there times that you forget that you are you?"

TIM: That's a fantastic question.

BENJAMIN: *(Reads)* "What do you mean?"

BARBARA: *(Reads)* "Do you become someone else? For instance, do you become Oscar Wilde in prison?" Pause.

BENJAMIN: *(Reads)* "I think I do. Become someone else. I mean I actually do become Oscar Wilde."

JANE: *(To RICHARD)* Telling the truth?

(RICHARD *shrugs.*)

BARBARA: *(Reads)* "As a person today, you seem very calm and easy going, you don't—there's not a lot of—you know—emotional things that I see. Big happiness, big sadness, you seem very very calm. Are you acting?" *(She looks up.)* Another pause. Benjamin you didn't answer. *(Reads)* Me again. "But on stage you show so much emotion, you know—you're like a different—like it just takes over."

BENJAMIN: *(Reads)* "Yes. It's not that I haven't got the capacity to feel and remember great emotions, um, I suppose that this period of my life corresponds—well not exactly to the period where Wilde was in prison…"

BARBARA: *(Reads)* "But it is *like* being in prison? Your amnesia."

BENJAMIN: *(Reads)* "In a way."

BARBARA: *(Reads)* "It's interesting to me that you connect the two. I don't want to put words in your mouth, but in a way, playing Oscar Wilde in prison has been a chance for you to express emotions that you feel?"

(Short pause)

(BENJAMIN reads to himself.)

BARBARA: Read it out loud, Uncle.

BENJAMIN: *(Reads)* "Very much so. Very much so."

JANE: My god—.

BARBARA: I know. I know. But he's not done.

BENJAMIN: *(Continues)* "As I say, I do believe—I don't mean to say I give the best performance that could ever be given—but I am Oscar Wilde when I do…." *(He reads to himself.)*

BARBARA: *(Gently)* Out loud, Uncle.

BENJAMIN: *(Reads)* "Not that I'm… No, in that sort of literal sexual sense that I've ever had that intensity of experience of love for a young man. I have had, not… well I suppose you could call it homosexual, certainly not homosexual in the sort of physical, complete sense, but I have had an intense—intense love—for a man, a young man— *(He is reading this just to himself now.)* "—I was young at the time— who was more or less my own age, somewhat older, but about three or four years older. So I can to that extent I can—I certainly feel no stranger to the idea of… loving a man intensely… I suppose it would be properly called, if you were asked to define it in sexual terms—a homosexual love. I don't mean a complete homosexual affair, but homosexual love. So I mean I have, as it were, that in common with Oscar Wilde." *(He suddenly stands, looks around.)* Can I smoke in here?

MARIAN: *(Giving him a cigarette)* No, Benjamin…

(BENJAMIN starts to head off with his copy of the transcript. Stops.)

BENJAMIN: *(To* BARBARA*)* Thank you. This is so interesting.

(BENJAMIN heads outside through the kitchen. They watch him go.)

(BARBARA turns on the tape recorder. Bad crackling sound of a piano. She stops it.)

BARBARA: I have just asked him if he wants to play me something on the piano. We've asked him this a hundred times, haven't we?

MARIAN: We have.

BARBARA: Marian's here. He sits down at the piano and he says—

(BARBARA turns on the tape recorder—a garbled voice.)

(BARBARA laughs.)

JANE: I couldn't understand.

(BARBARA stops the recorder.)

MARIAN: He said he's not use to this keyboard. *(Smiles, shakes her head.)* He hadn't played forever, and this is what he says….

BARBARA: And then…

(BARBARA starts the recorder and they and we hear BENJAMIN playing nicely but not perfectly Schubert's The Trout.)

JANE: That's him?

(*Lights fade.*)

Adam

(*Seconds later; the music on the tape recorder is still playing, but the phone in the kitchen has begun to ring.*)

JANE: I'll get it, Barbara. (*She starts to go.*) Anyone need anything? Tim knows this piece. Someday you should hear him sing.

(JANE *goes off. They listen.*)

BARBARA: (*To* TIM) You know this?

(*They listen and then* TIM *suddenly sings and sings well:*)

TIM: (*Sings*)
In einem Bächlein helle,
Da schoss in froher Eil
Die launische Forelle
Vorüber wei en Pfeil.

(*The others are taken aback:*)

TIM: I trained as a singer. I do musicals...I'm an actor and a singer... It's *The Trout*. It's well-known.

(JANE *returns.*)

JANE: (*Entering*) It's Adam.

MARIAN: (*Over this*) I'm not here. (*She stands to go off to her bedroom.*)

JANE: Don't run away. He's just on the phone. He's going to the concert. He just wants to let you know that. He wants to know if that's okay.

(MARIAN *doesn't say anything. Music on the recorder plays.*)

JANE: Is that okay? *(To* TIM*)* Were you just singing—.
(As she waits for a response:) He's says everyone's going.
(To BARBARA*)* What else is on the program tonight?

BARBARA: A group of kids playing fiddles. You know—
Suzuki. They're cute. They wear little red bandanas. A
few other singing groups. It's very—community. My
students put this together.

TIM: Did they.

JANE: Marian, what do I say? He's asking.

RICHARD: *(Suddenly standing)* Let me talk to him…

MARIAN: No, Richard!

BARBARA: Please—

RICHARD: For Christ sake, Marian—you paid for most
of that house. You built his fucking lawn business. And
now you're in Barbara's bedroom? And she's in her
fucking basement?!

MARIAN: *(Yelling)* No, Richard, no!

RICHARD: *(Over this)* Where are we—the Middle East?
Stand up for yourself. If you can't, that's where a
brother comes in. *(He heads off.)*

MARIAN: Richard!! *(Looks at the others)* What's he going
to do?

*(*BARBARA *shuts off the recorder and the music.)*

*(*BENJAMIN *has passed* RICHARD *on his way in.)*

JANE: Enjoy your cigarette, Uncle? You know those are
bad for you. Why start smoking now?

BENJAMIN: I've always smoked.

JANE: No, you haven't.

BENJAMIN: I remember always smoking.

JANE: *(Half to herself)* We remember what we want to
remember…

BARBARA: *(To* BENJAMIN*)* Sit down. You haven't finished your dinner. Marian, could you pass the potatoes and—

*(*MARIAN *suddenly gets up.)*

MARIAN: *(She heads for her bedroom, stops)* I asked Richard not to talk to him… Why can't he listen?! *(She hurries off.)*

BENJAMIN: *(To* TIM*)* I started smoking when I was twelve years old.

TIM: That's a really long time.

BARBARA: *(To* JANE*)* She saw Adam at church this morning. He didn't used to go to church, that's what she said.

JANE: What's he doing—stalking her? *(To* TIM*)* Adam said all these really nasty things to her. Blamed her. I don't think I've told you everything.

BARBARA: Sorry, Tim.

TIM: I'm fine. It must have been just awful.

JANE: *(To* BARBARA*)* I don't care if Adam was upset. What he said to her was unforgivable.

BARBARA: Evan was his daughter too. What's worse than losing a child? I don't know.

TIM: I can't imagine anything worse.

BARBARA: See, even Tim—.

TIM: "Even"—?

JANE: That doesn't justify what he said to her. We're talking about Evan's— "accident", Uncle. He blames our sister.

BENJAMIN: *(Confused)* For what?

JANE: For not answering her fucking phone! Marian didn't hear her phone. And so she's to blame... Never mind, Uncle. It's all in the past. It's done. Forget it.

BENJAMIN: *(Eating, to* BARBARA*)* What did Adam say?

BARBARA: Nothing, Uncle—

BENJAMIN: I don't understand.

JANE: Adam found Marian's cell, Uncle, in her purse. And there were some messages—

BARBARA: Three.

JANE: —from Evan, that she hadn't listened to. So she didn't hear her phone in her purse? Big fucking deal, Adam. *(To* TIM*)* He acted like a complete asshole to her. "Why the fuck didn't you answer your phone?" Like she killed her daughter!

BARBARA: Jane—.

JANE: That's what Marian heard! I don't want to see him tonight. I don't ever want to see the son of bitch. *(To* TIM*)* How many times do I not hear my phone? It's not like she did it on fucking purpose?

BARBARA: She did.

JANE: Did what?

BARBARA: Not answer when Evan called. On "fucking purpose".

JANE: I don't understand. That's not what you told me when—

BARBARA: They'd had a fight that morning. Evan and Marian. So she wasn't answering Evan's calls.

*(*JANE *is taken aback by this.)*

BARBARA: I didn't know this either until about a month ago. I haven't seen you in a month—.

JANE: On purpose—?

BARBARA: They'd had a fight. Not an uncommon thing between the two of them. You know that. Mothers and daughters, I guess. Some are more difficult than others. And so that day, she had decided she wouldn't answer Evan's calls. So it's not that she didn't hear them, like we first thought. *(Then)* That's why Adam… When she told him. I suppose he—got angry. Understandable. Isn't it? All this just came out one night—when we were still sharing my bedroom. She needed to talk… *(Silence)* She chose—not to answer her daughter.

JANE: Well, they'd had a fight.

BARBARA: And then she killed herself. Why? *(Shrugs)*

Anyway, I agree, Adam shouldn't have said half of what he said. It wasn't fair. And he knows that now. He's apologized to me—a hundred times. She won't talk to him. He keeps trying. *(Gestures toward the kitchen and the phone call. Shrugs)* Poor man. I've told them both that their daughter had many problems. I had her in high school… They'd done their damnedest. But they're not going to listen to me.

JANE: No.

BARBARA: They're just going to beat themselves up.

(RICHARD returns.)

RICHARD: *(Entering)* He's going to give her some money. A monthly check—the bastard didn't say how much.

BARBARA: She won't take it, Richard.

RICHARD: It's her god damn money…. Do you know how many years she kept his stupid lawn business afloat?

JANE: Richard, Barbara was just—.

BARBARA: Don't.

RICHARD: What?

JANE: Nothing.

RICHARD: *(Hesitates then)* She could get herself an apartment.

BARBARA: She doesn't want an—

RICHARD: What about you?

BARBARA: She's welcome here. I like having her here.

RICHARD: *(Sitting, to* JANE*)* On the phone she keeps complaining about what it's like living with Marian.

BARBARA: I mouth off. Don't take me seriously—.

JANE: *(To* BARBARA*)* You do?

BARBARA: I don't mean it—.

RICHARD: We can imagine what it must be like. *(To* JANE*)* Can't we?

JANE: I couldn't live with Marian.

BARBARA: It's just fine. The house is big enough.

RICHARD: It isn't, Barbara. *(Getting up)* Where is she?

BARBARA: Stay in here, Richard.

*(*RICHARD *looks at* BARBARA, *then sits back down.)*

RICHARD: *(To* JANE*)* He tried to give me all this bullshit about—how I just didn't understand.

JANE: Maybe you don't.

RICHARD: What do you mean? Of course I understand. I told him, I damn well understand. She's my sister. *(Starts to stand again)*

BARBARA: Stay in here. She'll come back when she's ready. You know Marian.

*(*RICHARD *sits back down.)*

BARBARA: And Richard, maybe she doesn't want you to help her. Maybe she needs to do this herself. Let's leave her alone.

(RICHARD *looks at* BARBARA.)

BARBARA: Eat some more. We made too much.

(Lights fade.)

Evan

(Lights up a short time later)

JANE: How is your eye, Richard?

BARBARA: What's wrong with your eye?

RICHARD: Nothing.

JANE: A little vein in his left eye—it what? Popped?

BARBARA: What does that mean?

JANE: That he now has blurred eyesight in his left eye.

BARBARA: Have you seen a doctor?

RICHARD: Of course I've seen a doctor. I'm fine.

BARBARA: Why didn't you tell me about this?

JANE: He's had two laser surgeries. They didn't help. He tries to compensate—watch how sometimes he closes that eye.

(BARBARA *studies* RICHARD.)

JANE: He's not going to do it when you stare at him. He asked if it could have been caused by stress. And his doctor— "oh yeah". He told me he thinks he knows the exact moment when the vein popped.

BARBARA: So it's like a stroke?

RICHARD: No.

JANE: *(Over this)* During a conversation with one fat ass Wall Street client.

BARBARA: *(Very concerned)* Richard….

RICHARD: It'll get better.

JANE: It's not going to get better. You told me that.

BARBARA: Twenty years in the Attorney General's office and you're the picture of health, and ten months in this place and he's having strokes.

RICHARD: *("Smiling")* There's a lawyer in the firm, his brother had something like this; and he'd been wearing glasses all of his life, and after just one surgery, he not only fixed the blurriness but no longer even needed glasses. *(Trying to make it all a joke)* Says it's really helped his golf game. So you never know.

BARBARA: You've taken up golf?

RICHARD: No.

BARBARA: *(To JANE)* Thank god.

(BENJAMIN is pouring himself another drink.)

BARBARA: Don't drink too much. You're acting today.

JANE: *(Getting up)* I'm going to see how Marian is. Maybe she shouldn't be alone, Barbara.

BARBARA: She's... *(Starts to stop her, then)* Go ahead.

(JANE goes off.)

BARBARA: *(To herself)* Go ahead...

(Short pause)

TIM: *(To say something)* You have a farmer's market.

BARBARA: What??

TIM: A farmer's market. In the village. In the parking lot.

BARBARA: Yes. Yes, we do.

TIM: *(Explaining)* I—passed it...

(BARBARA looks at her watch.)

RICHARD: Benjamin, do you need to prepare in any way?

BENJAMIN: For what?

BARBARA: You'll have to change your clothes.

(BENJAMIN *starts to stand.*)

BARBARA: You still have time.

BENJAMIN: I don't have to change my clothes?

BARBARA: Not yet.

TIM: *(Another try)* What a good idea, Barbara—to get your students involved today.

BARBARA: It was their idea—they wanted to do something. They're now my Seniors and so—they were— six, seven, eight years old when it happened? It's interesting what they remember. But it's been a part of who they are… *(Then)* At first I think they had in mind—something more— "exciting"? *(Smiles)* Like they saw when we killed Bin Laden. I said, I think this is about more than that. *(Then)* I assigned a poem—the one Benjamin, you're going to read—and to write an essay on— today. On the anniversary. On how we remember things. How we should remember. And two of my best students came up with this idea for a community concert. Instead of writing a paper. It was their idea.

TIM: *(Smiling)* Sounds like they just didn't want to write a paper. *(To* RICHARD*)* That's how I was—

BARBARA: No. No. You're wrong. *(Then)* The school at first didn't want to open the auditorium on a Sunday… But… It is a day you feel like you want to share with… With others. Do you feel that way?

TIM: I'm happy to be here—.

BARBARA: Even just sitting in an audience with others…

TIM: It sounds like a wonderful thing. I'm looking forward to it. And to you reading this mysterious poem, Benjamin.

RICHARD: Why is it mysterious?

TIM: They haven't told us what it is.

RICHARD: What's the poem, Barbara?

BARBARA: You'll have to wait until tonight. *(Standing)* Anyone still eating?

RICHARD: I might be done. And I might not be. Sit down.

(She sits)

RICHARD: Funny, it's one of those days, isn't it—where it comes in and out of your consciousness. Your head. The anniversary. This morning—with my friends. It was all about that. And then I forgot all about it. Then, it's back... *(Then to tim)* It's why Barbara came. To Rhinebeck. She came after the attacks. So I'll bet today you're having—.

BARBARA: There were a lot of reasons.

RICHARD: *(Over this)* She just picked up and left Manhattan.

BARBARA: I wasn't the only one.

RICHARD: *(To BARBARA)* Did you know I sent in a memorial plan?

BARBARA: What do you mean?

RICHARD: For the competition. I didn't tell you? I must have told Jane. Anyone could submit one.

TIM: I remember that.

RICHARD: Thousands of people did, I think. *(He smiles.)* I called mine a "peace garden". Later I read that something like four hundred submissions called theirs "peace gardens"...

TIM: What was it?

RICHARD: A garden maze… Places where you'd be in groups and then sections where only one person could fit, so you'd be alone… *(Shrugs)* I just wanted to do it. It felt good to do.

BARBARA: On T V it looked nice. What they ended up with. *(To* BENJAMIN*)* We watched a little this morning. Before we went to church. *(To* TIM *and* RICHARD*)* Lots of trees. Pools—in squares where the towers were.

RICHARD: Sort of. Not quite in the exact… Close enough.

BARBARA: *(To* BENJAMIN*)* The waterfalls? Remember? The bagpipes… Those school kids in their bright blue jackets? He liked the jackets.

RICHARD: We made them turn off the T Vs in the bar this morning. So we weren't watching. But somehow a full minute before—the exact time—we all knew. We felt it. There wasn't a sound. Then just the bells.

(JANE returns.)

JANE: She doesn't want to talk. She doesn't want company. She's lying on your bed, Barbara—

BARBARA: *(Over this)* Her bed.

JANE: Reading *Harry Potter. (Shakes her head, shrugs)* What are you talking about?

TIM: Richard submitted a plan for the ground zero memorial.

JANE: I think I knew that.

BARBARA: He didn't win.

JANE: I knew that.

TIM: I think if someone had asked me I'd have said— why not just a big statue to Phillipe Petit. That would be my memorial.

BARBARA: Who's—?

JANE: The French guy who tight-rope walked between the towers.

RICHARD: *(To* TIM*)* What does he have to do with—?

TIM: It's when the Trade Center—for a lot of people, I think, when it became—human. Up til then everybody hated those buildings. And—became glorious. My father was here then, doing something—a friend called him: "you're not going to believe this, get the hell downtown." Dad said he just watched this guy— between the two—walking. And it was beautiful. Like he'd conquered something inhuman, and tamed it for everyone. And made it human.

RICHARD: There was the guy who crawled up one of them-

TIM: That's right. I forgot about him. That's sort of the same thing.

RICHARD: So you'd have nothing about the attacks, the victims—

TIM: I don't know. I just think it would be inspiring. Phillipe Petit. It could be…

RICHARD: One of my buddies this morning at our breakfast—he had an idea. As crazy as yours.

TIM: I don't think mine's—.

RICHARD: He'd seen a show in Chelsea, an artist who'd done—what he called "candy spills". That's just what they were. Little wrapped candies, sort of spilled in a pile on the floor. And what you're supposed to do is—take one and eat it. And slowly then, over time, it'd all be gone. The pile is gone. *(Then)* He said the artist intended it as a memorial—for people dying of AIDS.

JANE: What do you mean? I don't understand—

RICHARD: I know. He said, the goal was to make
the world sweet again. *(Smiles)* And have everyone
participate. And—and this was most important—
he said the artist wanted to make art that would
disappear. That memorials are not in the past or the
future, but now. And so my friend, he was trying to
convince us that the best memorial for 9/11 would be
one that would have an end.

(Short pause)

JANE: Tim has a friend, a gay director. *(To* TIM*)* You
know who I mean? This made me think of him.
Graham. *(To the others)* Years ago—in the eighties, at
the height of the AIDS crisis for gay men, he's asked to
organize a fundraiser. *(To* TIM*)* You asked him—.

TIM: *(Continuing the story)* What sort of show could
he do? And Graham says, he's going to find the most
attractive "hot" boys he can, and have them strip.
And—be sexy as hell. *(Then)* I said—isn't that in sort
of bad taste? Given how people are dying? You know
what he said? That there are young boys right now,
who totally associate the act of sex with—death. And
isn't that wrong, he asked. How more wrong could
you be? Sex is not death; the exact opposite. And so he
wanted to memorialize the dead and the dying—with
sex. With life.

RICHARD: So he put on a strip show?

TIM: Yeah. *(As a joke)* And raised a hell of a lot of
money.

JANE: You won't believe how much money—

(They laugh; short pause.)

RICHARD: *(To* JANE*)* Barbara was saying that the kids
who are organizing today—they were six or seven
then... So pretty much their whole life...

JANE: Billy was twelve… I've asked him what he remembers.

RICHARD: What does Billy remember?

JANE: Well, I know he doesn't tell me everything. *(Then)* He said he remembers when I came to pick him up at school—there was a man, a father—his suit completely covered in dust. And how the man was checking his watch—to put down the "correct" time on a sheet in the school office. To sign his son out and take him home. I think what Billy was saying is that it seemed so normal on the one hand, and so—something else—on the other. At the same time. Unsettling for a kid. *(Shrugs)* And—this: I don't have any memory of this at all. About two years later, Billy just came out with this—how when we had stopped at an A T M, walking uptown—Billy says there was a long long line—and no one in that line was saying anything to anyone; no one was looking at anyone…

(Short pause)

BARBARA: Where were you, Tim?

TIM: In Boston. Doing a play.

BARBARA: You said. That song—.

TIM: Trying to reach people back in New York… That's what I remember. Making phone calls… Over and over again. Trying to…

JANE: Billy remembers the littler kids at school, later, drawing pictures of people with parachutes…

(Short pause)

RICHARD: I read that in the museum that they're building—whenever the hell they finish it.

TIM: Maybe another twenty years if they leave it to the 'politicians.'

RICHARD: It always ends up about money and real estate.

JANE: Do we really need a museum?

RICHARD: Anyway, there's going to be one, and it's going to have a display just about— *(Looks to* JANE *and* BARBARA*)* —those of you who lived downtown. Supposedly there's going to be a rack of discount Jeans—from Chelsea Jeans—remember Chelsea Jeans? —Amazingly preserved in all the dust from that day, from a shop window on Broadway. *(Then)* And they've got a recording of a teenager talking about how her family in Tribeca just wasn't going to leave. Her dad is saying, "Let's go to the supermarket." But there's no electricity. It's pitch dark. And everything in the refrigerator is melting all over the the floor…

TIM: Where were you, Benjamin? Do you remember?

BARBARA: He doesn't. *(To* BENJAMIN*)* You were making a movie in Bulgaria. One of those crazy places where they make movies to save money. You called me right away. I'd already made it to midtown. And by some amazing miracle my cell worked for you. *(To others)* I didn't know about Jane for almost a day. Richard called me and told me she was okay.

RICHARD: God, I remember.

BARBARA: I lied to Benjamin that whole day. *(To* BENJAMIN*)* You were too far away not to lie to. *(Smiles at him)*

JANE: *(To* TIM*)* Richard lost three people from his office…

RICHARD: They're the ones we toast—at our breakfasts—every year… This morning.

BARBARA: We're a hundred miles away up here, and this morning at church—it was a surprisingly long list

of names… *(New thought)* We found some notebooks—
appointment books is really what they are.

RICHARD: What are you talking about?

BARBARA: Do you know what I'm talking about, Uncle?

BENJAMIN: What?

BARBARA: *(To* RICHARD*)* In a bookshop. In a barn
up here. We found them in a drawer with a lot of
junk. Someone had— "lost" them I guess. For '99,
2000, 2001… They kind of end on September 10th…
(To BENJAMIN*)* We've spent hours together looking
through them… He doesn't remember.

JANE: *What* are they??

RICHARD: I don't understand.

BARBARA: *(She starts to get up)* I can get them if you—I'll
show you. They're in the living room. *(She hurries off.)*

RICHARD: *(Calls)* What sort of…?

JANE: Notebooks, she said. Appointment books?
(Shrugs) More mysteries, Uncle….

TIM: About eight or ten days after—. So maybe like
September 20th. I'm back from Boston. Everything
was still so—fresh. And the subways, we were still all
scared. Well, a couple of friends of mine, writers, and I
got together for lunch. *(Then, connecting to the previous
conversation)* At Un Deux Trois. Next to the Belasco.

RICHARD: I know where that—.

JANE: *(To* TIM*)* What are you going to say?

TIM: I don't think I've told you this. *(To* RICHARD*)* As
you said, things keep coming in and out. *(Points to
his head. Continues)* The three of us made a rule—for
the entire lunch we could only talk about theater or
books or films—only about Art. Not a word about…
what had happened. And—there were some very long

pauses… *(Smiles)* But… One of my friends is really into Yiddish plays. He thinks there are all these great unknown plays out there from years ago, now lost. Anyway, he told us a story at this lunch. A young Yiddish student some years ago, he's having trouble finding books in Yiddish to study. So he puts up signs in neighborhoods like Brighton Beach, the Upper West Side— "Yiddish scholar seeking Yiddish books." *(Then:)* Calls start to come. For one "book pick-up" — he borrows a little van, drives to Brooklyn, pulls up in front of an old apartment building; rings a buzzer, goes in, an old man appears at the door, takes him inside and shows him boxes and boxes of Yiddish books. *(Then:)* The young man is obviously pleased, and starts to lift one of the boxes. But the man stops him. What are you doing? He asks. I'm taking the boxes to my van. Wait, says the old man, first—I must tell you about each book.

(JANE smiles, looks at RICHARD, who is absorbed in the story.)

TIM: So now after many hours, the young man's finally got the books in the van. He goes to shake the man's hand, and the old man says again, What are you doing? I have to get home with the van, this van is borrowed. Then the old man, gesturing to the whole eight or nine-story apartment building, says, "But I've told my neighbors you were coming, and they all have Yiddish books for you…". *(He is moved, tries not to cry.)* The young man thought those books had been lost. But they weren't. *(Then)* I don't know why, I still want to cry. Those days right after…

JANE: I remember.

(BARBARA has entered, with a small pile of little notebooks— appointment diaries. She is confused:)

JANE: Tim was telling us about some wonderful books being saved.

TIM: More than just…

JANE: Are those the notebooks, Barbara?

(MARIAN *then appears right behind* BARBARA *and this gets everyone's attention.*)

BARBARA: (*About the notebooks, taking them to the table*) We've figured out that he's an accountant. The owner of these. (*To* MARIAN) Didn't we, Marian?

(*Everyone looks to* MARIAN *who nods.*)

BARBARA: His office is on Park Place.

RICHARD: Where the mosque was going to be.

BARBARA: Was that where it was? (*Showing the notebooks*) You can see what I mean here—in 2001—.

(*They start to get up to look.*)

BARBARA: I'll pass them around. (*Continues*) He writes down his appointments, and his habit is to cross them off when he's had them. Even lunches. Shows. (*To* TIM *and* BENJAMIN) He went to the theater a lot. Marian, come and join us.

(*Then about the books. As* MARIAN *sits*)

BARBARA: They stop being crossed off here… Sept. 10th. After that, nothing is crossed off… And slowly there are no more appointments. A dentist appointment in December. Which he obviously did not keep.

JANE: (*To* MARIAN) We've been talking about—.

BARBARA: I told her. (*To* MARIAN) You were already at school, I think. Weren't you? That morning.

(MARIAN *nods.*)

BARBARA: I think you told me you tried to keep the news from your kids as long as possible.

MARIAN: I did.

JANE: They're just second graders.

BARBARA: *(About a notebook entry)* Look here, he saw *Phantom of the Opera* on May 22. He went with "Joan". Then the next weekend, Memorial Day weekend, he obviously stayed in the city—there's a brunch. This restaurant still exists. I looked it up online. And then Marian discovered… Show them. *(She hands MARIAN one of the notebooks.)* Here—tell them…

MARIAN: *(Hesitates, then explains her discovery)* In 1998, he had dinner here with "Joan" as well. The only two times in the books we could find. For some reason that seemed interesting. Some place on 23rd Street. He put his name in the back of this one: George Satterlee.

RICHARD: *(Repeats)* "Satterlee." *(He doesn't know a Satterlee.)*

BARBARA: Here. This is what I wanted you to see. Sept. 11th. Not crossed out. "Breakfast." "WOW."

RICHARD: "WOW"?

TIM: I'd say "WOW" is right…

BARBARA: We figured it meant "Windows on the World".

(Short pause)

JANE: How did these get—?

BARBARA: They just sell whole libraries and… Estates do. And they have to take away everything. Maybe. *(To MARIAN)* We bought these at the Book Barn in Hillsdale? Didn't we?

TIM: Amazing where things end up…

JANE: *(To TIM)* Maybe he saw a show you were in. That would be incredible, wouldn't it? That he'd have been in your audience?

(Pause, as they all look, turning pages)

JANE: *(Still looking)* So interesting. Like you're eavesdropping. Sometimes I like to go to restaurants by myself—you hear so much that way. People act like you're not even there. Just look down at a book, and they'll say anything right in front of you... Right next to you.

(As they look at the books.)

RICHARD: *(To* MARIAN*)* How's *Harry Potter?*

BARBARA: *(To* RICHARD*)* It was Evan's... *(To* MARIAN*)* She read them all, didn't she?

*(*MARIAN *nods.)*

BARBARA: Marian hadn't read them. So she asked me to get them from—her home. How many do you have left?

MARIAN: I've read all of them now. At least once.

BARBARA: When Evan was—. When she was how old? *(Continues, as they all look at the books)* About eleven I think. Marian and I—I don't know how you got me to do this.

MARIAN: *(Looking at another book)* You wanted to. I didn't.

JANE: What?

BARBARA: *(To* MARIAN*)* That's not how I remember it. *(Continuing, they continue to look through the books)* Oblong was having one of those midnight parties for the publication of one of the *Harry Potters.* And Marian got us to dress as witches. *(Smiles)* Marian had taught every kid who was there. *(Then)* Evan then sat and read the book, I don't think she slept for three days. Did she?

(They look at the notebooks.)

MARIAN: *(To* RICHARD*)* What did Adam say?

RICHARD: *(Hesitates, looks at his sisters, then)* He didn't say much. We didn't talk that long.

MARIAN: Is he coming to the concert?

RICHARD: I don't think so.

BARBARA: Marian forgets. Sometimes she's worse than you, Benjamin. *(Pats* BENJAMIN*'s hand)* Even last Christmas she and Evan—she got Evan to do this together—they sewed things for the Sinterklaas Parade.

TIM: *(To* JANE*)* What's Sinterklaas—?

JANE: A Rhinebeck thing.

BARBARA: Evan told me what fun that was. And *('to the others')* it wasn't me, it was Marian who insisted on us dressing as witches for the *Harry Potter.* She forgets that. Evan would pretend that she was embarrassed? But you could tell she thought—what a neat Mom I've got. And she was right. And every kid there—you could tell how much Marian had meant to each one. *(Then:)* Just this Christmas Evan gave her Mother a C D mix of music she liked. *(To* MARIAN*)* How many times did you play that? *(To the others)* Every time we were in the car together, she had to play that. She went online, and got the lyrics to these— "songs" —and she learned them. Didn't you? *(She stares at* MARIAN.*)* Don't forget that. Don't let yourself forget any of that. *(Then:)* Benjamin, maybe you should get changed.

BENJAMIN: Can I have a cigarette first?

MARIAN: No. No, you can't. You've smoked enough.

BARBARA: Your suit's on your bed. Let us know if you need any help.

BENJAMIN: I don't need help. Why am I changing?

BARBARA: For your performance.

BENJAMIN: I'm doing a performance?

(BENJAMIN *goes; they continue to look at the notebooks.*)

TIM: Can I see that notebook, Richard?

JANE: *(After watching* BENJAMIN *go)* He's such a mystery, our Uncle. What is going on in that head of yours? I think he knows everything and is just keeping it all to himself.

MARIAN: Barbara sometimes calls him "Buddha".

JANE: I like that. Buddha. When he comes back I'll rub his stomach for good luck.

BARBARA: He never gets angry. Why doesn't he just say, "this is terrible"? "I can't function properly." Only once, and that was when he'd just come to live with me. That's the only time I have ever heard him say, "help me". *(Standing)* What about dessert. Vanilla ice cream and cake? Should I just bring it all out? *(She starts picking up plates.)*

JANE: *(Getting up)* Let me help.

TIM: *(Standing)* I can help. I'm not a guest. I don't consider myself a guest.

RICHARD: *(Trying to make a joke)* I think Tim has earned those stripes.

BARBARA: Why don't you help too, Richard. You could use a few more stripes.

(They all pick up things.)

BARBARA: It's store-bought cake; I didn't make it. *(She goes off with plates, etc.)*

(As the others clean up:)

TIM: *(To say something)* What's—a Sinterklaas Parade?

RICHARD: Santa Claus.

TIM: I'd guessed that much.

MARIAN: They have giant puppets, and they have a parade and candles—it's beautiful. Sinterklaas rides a white horse...

TIM: Sounds great. Like a show... *(He follows* MARIAN *off.)*

JANE: *(To* RICHARD*)* Here, take these... Do something.

*(*RICHARD *takes a few bowls and heads off.)*

(In the distance church bells are playing a tune.)

BARBARA: *(Entering, passing Richard, listening to the bells, to herself)* What are they playing now? *(To* JANE*, piling plates)* Is that what I think it is?

JANE: What?

BARBARA: *(To herself, listening)* "Onward Christian Soldiers". *(Explaining to* JANE*)* Those "bells". The church. They started playing that yesterday. I couldn't believe it.

*(*JANE *is heading off)*

BARBARA: Close the back door, would you, Jane? Just close it.

*(*JANE *goes off, carrying dishes, and to close the door.)*

RICHARD: *(Entering with* TIM*)* The Sinterklaas Parade is *one* day a year—. You don't have to move up here to see it.

TIM: It just doesn't feel like I want to be there anymore. Obviously, I'm not talking about just a parade.

(Off the bells are silenced.)

BARBARA: *(To herself about the bells)* Thank god... Peace...

*(*MARIAN *returns with the cake.)*

TIM: *(To* RICHARD*)* Do you know *The Visit*? It's a play.

RICHARD: I'm a lawyer, Tim...

MARIAN: *(To the women)* We still need the ice cream…
(She heads off.)

BARBARA: *(To* MARIAN*)* Marian, *Onward Christian
Soldiers.* Today of all days…

*(*JANE *returns with a wine bottle.)*

JANE: Richard, your wine.

TIM: Do you need the—?

JANE: It's twist off.

TIM: *(Continuing)* In this play, *The Visit,* a woman, a
billionaire comes back to her old town that's going
through tough times. She's got a grudge against one of
the citizens, a man who years ago dumped her.

*(*JANE *and* BARBARA *serve the cake.)*

JANE: Tim—

TIM: *(To* JANE*)* I'm trying to explain to Richard, what
I'm feeling.

RICHARD: I don't even like the theater, Tim.

TIM: *(Continues)* So this billionaire says to the
citizens, she'll make them all rich. Pay all their debts,
everything. The catch is—she wants them to execute
the guy who dumped her. Of course everyone is
shocked and says no, no, we couldn't… But then,
pretty soon they start measuring his neck for a noose.

*(*MARIAN *has returned with the ice cream and a scoop. And
she is serving.)*

(Then his point:)

TIM: She's Bloomberg. That's what the city's become.
He's bought us.

MARIAN: *(Confused, still serving)* What? I don't
understand.

TIM: Fucking Bloomberg.

BARBARA: He hates Bloomberg.

(MARIAN *just shrugs. Serving:*)

BARBARA: Aren't you exaggerating a little, Tim? Bloomberg hasn't asked anyone to *kill* anyone.

JANE: Not yet.

RICHARD: I see what you're saying now.

TIM: I used to love the city. And we only have ourselves to blame.

RICHARD: You don't need a play to tell you that.

BARBARA: Maybe if you got out of Manhattan...

TIM: That's what I'm saying—

JANE: Tim has too good a deal to do that.

TIM: My lease is now my greatest financial asset. Maybe my only—

BARBARA: What do you mean?

JANE: He's been in Manhattan Plaza for years. The rent's tied to his earnings—.

TIM: *(Smiles)* I can't leave.

JANE: We *talk* about leaving all the time.

TIM: I look at here, Rhinebeck. I think...

BARBARA: Rhinebeck's got its share of problems too.

MARIAN: Evan hated Rhinebeck. I don't know why.

(Short pause. The ice cream and cake is ready.)

BARBARA: Shall we sit down?

(They begin to sit down.)

RICHARD: Evan probably hated—lots of things.

JANE: *(To* BARBARA*)* You think Benjamin's all right—

MARIAN: He's not a child. He knows how to dress himself, Jane.

(They all are seated now. As they begin to eat their ice cream:)

TIM: *(back to talking about New York)* I wait on rich people every day in the city. There seems to be a whole lot of them now. How did that happen? *(He eats.)* They give off this—I don't know what.

JANE: Smell?

(Laughter)

BARBARA: Jane…

TIM: Aura. The sense that they think they've really earned what they've got. There are times when I—I see myself in the mirror behind the bar, waiting for an order, and I'm standing there with two or three other waiters—also actors, brilliant fucking actors… I'm forty-three. And start to feel like a fool.

MARIAN: You're only forty-three? Jane, he's—forty-three. *(To TIM)* You know Jane isn't forty-three.

JANE: He knows. *(back to the city:)* It makes me angry, those people. After a while it just eats you up. Turns you in on yourself. Just eats and eats… What Tim and I could do with what some of them spend on one fucking bottle of wine.

(RICHARD reaches to pour his wine.)

RICHARD: I didn't spend that much.

BARBARA: Are we going to have coffee?

JANE: *(Standing)* I'll put it on. Coffee or decaf?

(They want coffee. JANE starts to go, then stops.)

JANE: *(Continuing)* You'd think there would be some—humility.

RICHARD: I don't know why she'd think that?

(JANE goes off to the kitchen.)

BARBARA: *(Calls)* It's all ready, you just have to add the water.

BARBARA: *(To* RICHARD*)* Jane's asked Uncle for a loan, Richard. A few thousand. I think he can afford it. What do you think?

RICHARD: I think so. I think he can. *(Noticing* TIM's *discomfort)* Sorry, Tim—

TIM: No, no. It's fine.

(They eat.)

RICHARD: *(To Tim, back to New York)* A lawyer in my firm, he's always saying about New York— *(He tastes the icing on the cake.)* —look at the elections. He took me to a website. Shows how people vote—every district, across the country. *(Eats)* In Manhattan, pretty much every race is won by something like—ninety-two percent, ninety, ninety-five percent. Always by the Democrats of course. Only last election, Rangel, he got a little less. Think what we'd say if someone like him, in the South say or way out West, someplace we ridicule, if someone who had been accused and full of bullshit, if in the middle of all that, they elected him with eighty-five percent of the vote. And we did. *(Shrugs, then)* He was my Congressman. Hardly anyone even seems embarrassed. We moved to Brooklyn.

MARIAN: That wasn't the only reason, Pamela wanted—

*(*JANE *returns.)*

JANE: Coffee's on.

*(*TIM *looks at her)*

JANE: What?

BARBARA: *(Eating)* Is today really a day to talk politics?

RICHARD: *(Ignoring her, to* TIM*)* Cuomo's not as bad as I thought he'd be. I'm really surprised.

TIM: Me too. But we'll see.

RICHARD: We're just talking about the city, Barbara. *(Continuing, to* TIM*)* We went through the whole map on this website and the only other place that even comes close to such lopsided elections—northern Texas. *(Eat)* You can swing a dead cat on the corner of Broadway and 72nd and have about the same chance of hitting a Republican as winning the lotto. In lots of ways, New York has to be one of the most parochial places in the country.

MARIAN: *(Eating)* Do you now believe everything your rich Republican friends tell you? Mother, father, close your ears.

RICHARD: I don't know where I am going politically, Marian. I know I've—jumped. Just jumped. I'm waiting to see where I land. If I land. *(Eats)*

JANE: What difference does it make what we are now? A Wall Street sponsored Republican or a Wall Street sponsored Democrat? *(Mocking)* "Oh which side will I be on?"

BARBARA: I thought you were just talking about the city—.

JANE: Tell me, am I the only one here who wakes up almost every morning, and as I am trying to convince myself to get out of bed, I'm thinking— "We're fucked."

(Laughter)

TIM: I feel—. [like that]

JANE: *(Patting his head, like to a child)* I know you feel the same way, dear. I know. I see how you look every morning...*(To the others)* He's been reading a book.

I tell him don't read that book the first thing in the morning. And don't read it right before you're trying to go to sleep.

RICHARD: What book?

JANE: He comes out of the bedroom—every morning now—after reading a chapter, all red in the face, just stands there. puts his finger to his head—like it's a gun and "shoots".

(Laughter)

BARBARA: *(Laughing)* Good thing it's only his finger.

TIM: *(Out of the laughter)* We tried to sell the Pennsylvania Turnpike to Abu Dhabi.

BARBARA: What??

JANE: It's from that book—.

MARIAN: Who was trying to sell the—?

TIM: The State of Pennsylvania.

RICHARD: I heard about this.

BARBARA: Why?

JANE: *(It's obvious:)* Because they're broke, Barbara.

TIM: *(Eating)* And Chicago's already sold a fifty-year lease to all of its parking meters—to a Middle East hedge fund. So if you want to have a block party in Chicago now and need to close down a street for a few hours? Like say on the 4th of July to celebrate American Independence Day? So you can have maybe a fucking parade with someone dressed up as—let's say—George fucking Washington? You have to get permission first from an Arab Sheik.

MARIAN: Is that really true?

TIM: Sometimes the only voice I hear in my head sounds like—Lewis Black. There is so much we're not talking about.

(Pause. They eat.)

BARBARA: Well—I like Elizabeth Warren…

(This gets everyone animated; others: "Me too." "I do too.")

BARBARA: Who else? Who else do we like?

TIM: Cuomo, sort of. I'm not convinced yet.

RICHARD: We'll see.

JANE: We already said him. Who else? Anyone else?

(No one else.)

RICHARD: I've never seen this country more brutal.

JANE: Is it "brutal"?

RICHARD: Maybe that isn't the word—maybe lost?

TIM: Lost. That's true.

JANE: And how they keep us wound up and divided. At the same time.

RICHARD: I see them every day—even with a bad eye you can see it—big fucking law firms—like my big fucking law firm— "fix" our so-called reforms.

TIM: Maybe—. You know how on your income tax there's a little box if you want a few bucks to go to pay for Presidential elections—

JANE: Which no one is going to take anymore—. Not after our guy—.

TIM: *(Continues)* That little box you can check—which is completely meaningless, isn't it?

RICHARD: It is.

BARBARA: I check it off every year.

TIM: Does anyone in the government even look at those little check marks? Do we really think someone is counting them up? *(Smiles)*

JANE: *(Holding up his hand)* I'll take that job.

(Laughter)

JANE: Seriously, Billy would take it.

TIM: Just more bullshit. Anyway, maybe all they need to do to make us feel even better—is just add a few more boxes for us to check.

RICHARD: Good idea. Very good idea.

TIM: That would make me feel better.

JANE: Me too!

RICHARD: A box say for—do you want two dollars of your tax to go to buy back—the Pennsylvania Turnpike!

(Laughter, they are having fun.)

JANE: "But we own that, don't we?"

(More laugther, then:)

BARBARA: *(It just comes out)* Why has our government given money to the families of 9/11?

(Everyone except MARIAN *is taken aback by this.)*

RICHARD: What?

BARBARA: I'm asking a question. I've been thinking about this.

JANE: Why we've given—?

BARBARA: Yes. *(She looks at* MARIAN.*)*

MARIAN: We've talked about this.

RICHARD: Where did this come from?

BARBARA: It's been on my mind all day. Watching T V this morning. It's been on my mind. Can I ask the question? Am I permitted to ask the question? It's just us. The door's closed.

RICHARD: Okay…

BARBARA: *That's* something I never hear anyone talking about. You were saying people don't talk about things. I don't mean those who—the responders. And I'm not talking about those with medical problems and helping them—after they were told 'it's okay, it's okay,' then— well actually it wasn't. *(Then, after a look at* MARIAN*)* This is all right?

JANE: Yes.

BARBARA: I mean— just the families of people who died. Why has the government paid *them*?

MARIAN: *(Explaining to the others)* One of Barbara's students asked her that.

BARBARA: She asked in class—and I had to stop a couple of students from yelling at her. I'm sure once they were out of class...I told her I'd think about it. And ask around. What do you think? Why are we giving them money? *(Then:)* When a plane crashes or there's a car accident or someone is shot in the street by a robber—the government doesn't give their families money. Does it? Do we?

JANE: But insurance companies—.

BARBARA: Not the government.

RICHARD: I see. I understand the question. The Gulf coast—that was insurance companies... What this student is asking is— why was this different, with the 9/11 families? Good question. Oklahoma City. Very good question. I don't know.

(Pause)

TIM: I've been asked a similar question. A friend of a friend lost her daughter in the attack. I remember being surprised when she said to me—you know my daughter was a victim, why do they call her a hero?

(Then:)

RICHARD: I suppose— "we've" needed to call people "heroes" to justify—. *(Then)* With "victims" —well for them, you just hunt down the "criminals". And bring them to "justice". But that's not all we've been doing, is it? We've been at war. A war on terror. What the hell does that mean?

BARBARA: Obama stopped using that—.

TIM: So he stopped using the name, Barbara.

RICHARD: He had his chance to denounce all this— crap. And he said he would. And then he didn't. Do we still believe in trials? Do we really think torturers should go unpunished? I'd ask our President that. *(Then)* Are principles compromised—any longer "principles"?

BARBARA: He got Bin Laden...

(Short pause)

RICHARD: But to shoot him, unarmed, in the head. It sounds like he didn't even resist. Why do that? Because we're scared??

JANE: How did they know he was unarmed?

MARIAN: I'm happy he's dead, Richard.

RICHARD: So am I. But I also think it's sad that we're that scared.

MARIAN: Aren't you scared, Richard?

RICHARD: I had to get out of the city today. The whole run up to this day—others have kept telling us what we need to feel. What I should feel. This morning with my buddies, normally, in past years, we'd take half a day or more, and crawl home. *(Smiles)* But today you felt the difference. The noise. And I don't mean just the crowds. I mean the noise. Suddenly one of my buddies just said, 'haven't we done this long enough? Can't we stop now!'

(Short pause)

JANE: I'll get the coffee... *(Stands)*

RICHARD: *(To* BARBARA*)* So what are you going to tell your student?

BARBARA: Not that. *(Then)* Not that, Richard. *(Then)* I can't tell these kids that politicians are all corrupt or complicit or just trying to keep their jobs, and elections are pretty much meaningless. Or that real estate interests control everything in the city. Or—all those other things. I'm not going to tell my kids that. *(Then)* I asked Benjamin for advice.

JANE: Benjamin?

BARBARA: He's good to talk things through with. And you can say the stupidest thing and you know he'll forget it.

MARIAN: And he's a very good listener.

BARBARA: That morning, I had friends die. I had a neighbor... I couldn't even begin now to tell you what I saw, and what I still see... Things out of hell. *(Then)* I described it all to Benjamin. *(Then)* I decided that this was a big and important subject to discuss with students. My best students. Seniors. Going out into the world. And I felt—this question, it was really only one of so many questions. That I could ask them. That I have. So—I started to make a list. I made a list. Marian's heard all this. *(She nods.)* I'll tell you.

JANE: Please... *(She sits back down.)*

BARBARA: I know it by heart. The list: *(The list:)* Are they heroes, those people who tragically died? What does that mean? *(Continues the list:)* Is a memorial for the dead or the living? *(Then:)* Some questions are pretty... *(To* RICHARD*)* They're kids...

RICHARD: I understand...

BARBARA: Marian's heard all this... *(Continues:)* Why would someone—and I'll expand this to include more than 9/11—why would a human being strap a bomb to his waist, his chest, or his feet, or stuff it down his crotch and then go out to find the biggest crowd of strangers to blow up? *(Continues)* Has this sort of killing ever occurred before in the history of the human race? "Suicide bombers" — when did we first hear this phrase? *(Continues. Smiles)* Let's spend the hour today class, talking about—the meaning of this word, "compensation". How do we compensate for the loss of life? The loss of security? The loss of confidence? Or—a new one I thought of today, Richard.

RICHARD: What?

BARBARA: How do we compensate for the loss of sight? Or vision. Does our other eye compensate and get stronger?

RICHARD: Do we just see less?

BARBARA: And—as they've all met Benjamin, he's come to a few classes. I've had most of the students here for one reason or another. In fact it was their idea to get him to read today. So this question: how does one compensate for the loss of memory?

JANE: Are there times when it's better to forget?

(Short pause)

BARBARA: Why do young people kill themselves?

MARIAN: I asked her to ask that.

BARBARA: I'm not saying they'll tell us. Or can. Or even that they know. But we can talk about it. Can't we? We can at least ask the question.

TIM: And so many of these bombers are also young men and women.

BARBARA: We'll take on one of these each day. We'll spend the whole hour on it. Maybe the kids will have some answers... *(Continues)* Do you ever feel you can't express your feelings, or speak about what you've seen? *(Then:)* What you read and see on T V, does it or does it not reflect the world you live in?

(Lights fade.)

Dressing The Wound

(A short time later; BENJAMIN enters, now dressed in a suit; his tie crooked; he holds a book.)

BENJAMIN: What am I doing?

(They laugh.)

JANE: Uncle, you look wonderful. He looks fantastic.

BARBARA: His tie's crooked—. *(She goes to straighten it.)*

RICHARD: Are we dressing up? I didn't bring anything-

MARIAN: It's casual. You look fine. *(To BARBARA)* Isn't it?

BARBARA: *(Of course)* It's at the high school. *(To BENJAMIN)* You found the book. *(To MARIAN)* I left it on top of his suit.

JANE: He looks so good. Tim, doesn't he look good? You look so handsome!

BENJAMIN: What the hell am I doing?

(They laugh.)

JANE: You're going to act, Uncle. You're going back on stage!

BARBARA: *(Fixing his tie)* You're giving a reading, Benjamin. Remember? We've been rehearsing all week. For 9/11. Today is its tenth anniversary.

RICHARD: What are you going to read, Uncle?

BENJAMIN: I don't know.

BARBARA: *(Still fixing the tie)* You know. We've been practicing.

RICHARD: Is that it in there? In that book?

BENJAMIN: *(To BARBARA)* Is it?

BARBARA: I want it to be a surprise for them. Though I think they probably know it... *(About the tie)* There, that's better. Did you shave?

BENJAMIN: I shaved this morning.

JANE: He looks good, Barbara.

BENJAMIN: *(Opening the book)* What am I reading?

BARBARA: It's bookmarked—.

JANE: Don't you want to read it to us—to practice, Uncle?

BARBARA: Jane, I want it to be—.

TIM: A dress rehearsal.

BARBARA: Tim. *(Looking for help)* Marian—

MARIAN: Let him read it, Barbara.

BENJAMIN: Maybe I should... *(Looking through the book)* Where's...?

BARBARA: It's marked. Here.... *(Shows him)* I really wanted it to be a surprise—.

JANE: *(Over this)* Come on, he should practice, Barbara—.

BARBARA: We've been practicing. You just haven't been here to help him!

(This stops everyone. BARBARA composes herself.)

BARBARA: Maybe a little rehearsal would be a good thing. A friendly audience, Uncle.

TIM: The high school audience won't be—

JANE: *(To* TIM*)* Shsh.

BARBARA: What do *you* want to do, Uncle?

BENJAMIN: What am I doing??

MARIAN: *(Taking charge)* You're going to read this— *(Points out)* poem... To us. As practice. *(To others)* Barbara's edited it a little...

*(*BENJAMIN *looks at the poem.)*

BARBARA: *(To* MARIAN*)* It's like he's never seen it before.

MARIAN: Every afternoon this whole week Barbara and Benjamin have been practicing this. The patience this woman has...

RICHARD: We know...

BARBARA: Come on, I'm sorry I said—.

JANE: Of a saint.

BARBARA: I'm not a saint...

MARIAN: She was telling me that a student found a D V D of one of Uncle's movies and they showed it after school. They asked Benjamin to come and talk about it... Sign autographs. *(Smiles)*

JANE: That must have made you feel good, Uncle.

BENJAMIN: *(He's been reading the poem to himself)* What?

BARBARA: I think it did. I hope so. *(To* BENJAMIN*)* Go ahead... They're insisting, Uncle. Read it. Do you know where to start? My god, we've been rehearsing this. *(Points)* There... *(To others)* It's Whitman...*The Wound Dresser.*

BENJAMIN: I should read?

BARBARA: Yes! Read it.

BENJAMIN: *(Reads)* "An old man—.

BARBARA: Speak up. Come on, you know better.

(BENJAMIN *looks at* BARBARA.)

BENJAMIN: *(Louder)* "An old man—.

BARBARA: That's right. Go ahead and read.

BENJAMIN: *(Reading)*
"An old man bending I come among new faces,

JANE: Sit down. Shouldn't we sit down?

BARBARA: We have to go soon.

TIM: *(To others, over this)* So we're more like an audience.

(*As they move chairs, etc and sit.*)

MARIAN: *(To* BENJAMIN*)* Sit here, Uncle. You're going to be sitting on stage tonight.

(BENJAMIN *looks to* BARBARA*)*

BENJAMIN: Barbara?

BARBARA: Go ahead, Benjamin. Go ahead. We can use the practice.

JANE: What's it about? I forget.

RICHARD: *(To* JANE, *over this)* Whitman working in hospitals. During the Civil War.

(BENJAMIN *sits, then looks up.*)

BENJAMIN: *(Explaining)* I haven't memorized it.

(*They laugh, he smiles.*)

BARBARA: *(Smiling at his joke)* Just read, will you?

BENJAMIN: *(Reads)*
"An old man bending I come among new faces,
Years looking backward resuming in answer to
  children,
Come tell us old man…
But in silence, in dreams' projections,

Bearing the bandages, water and sponge,
Straight and swift to my wounded I go,
Where they lie on the ground after the battle brought
  in,
Where their priceless blood reddens the grass the
  ground...

(BENJAMIN *turns two pages by mistake and is confused.*
BARBARA *Sees this, and goes to help him.*)

BARBARA: *(Explaining)* You turned two pages...

(BARBARA *stands by* BENJAMIN *as he continues. As he
reads, she will walk around the room, sharing looks with
everyone.*)

BENJAMIN:
"From the stump of the arm, the amputated hand,
I undo the clotted lint, remove the slough, wash off the
  matter and the blood,
Back on his pillow the soldier bends...
His eyes are closed, his face is pale, he dares not look
  on the bloody stump,
And has not yet look'd on it.

JANE: *(To* BARBARA*)* Thank you, Barbara.

BENJAMIN: "I dress a wound in the side, deep, deep...
I dress the perforated shoulder, the foot with bullet-
  wound,
Cleanse the one with the gnawing and putrid
  gangrene...

RICHARD: *(To* BARBARA, *offering his chair)* Barbara?

(BARBARA *shakes her head.*)

BENJAMIN: "I am faithful, I do not give out,
The fractur'd thigh, the knee, the wound in the
  abdomen,
These and more I dress with impassive hand,
(yet deep in my breast afire, a burning flame.)

BARBARA: *(To* MARIAN*)* Do you mind?

*(*MARIAN *scoots over, and* BARBARA *sits with* MARIAN *on the floor.)*

BENJAMIN: "Thus in silence in dreams' projections,
Returning, resuming, I thread my way through the
   hospitals,
The hurt and wounded I pacify with soothing hand,
I sit by the restless
(He stops briefly and looks at the others.)
"I sit by the restless all the dark night, some are so
   young,
Some suffer so much...

*(*MARIAN *puts her arm around* BARBARA*, and holds her. others notice this.)*

BENJAMIN: "I recall the experience—sweet and sad.
"Many a soldier's loving arms about this neck have
   cross'd and rested
Many a soldier's kiss dwells on these bearded lips."
(He closes the book. Seriously, to BARBARA*)* Should I have
grown a beard?

(This makes them all laugh.)

BARBARA: *(Trying not to cry)* No, no... You're fine as
you are, Uncle... *(Then:)* That was good. Do it like
that...

(No one knows what to do.)

BARBARA: We should probably straighten up a little bit
and go. You want to get good seats.

(They begin to stand.)

JANE: I left a sweater in Barbara's car...

TIM: I'll get it. *(To* BARBARA*)* It's not locked?

BARBARA: *(Answering: of course not)* This is Rhinebeck.

MARIAN: I lock my car.

(TIM *goes.*)

(*They begin to pick up things.*)

JANE: (*To* BENJAMIN) When you read, it's like your old self… The performing self comes out. Do you like that? Do you enjoy that?

BENJAMIN: I do.

BARBARA: (*To* JANE) I'll pull out your couch, Jane.

MARIAN: I can do it. You can't do everything. And I'll get sheets and pillows. (*She goes into the living room.*)

BARBARA: (*Calling after her*) And towels.

JANE: (*To* BARBARA) This must be very satisfying for you.

BARBARA: I think it is. Especially when he remembers things. (*To* BENJAMIN) You do remember some things, don't you?

BENJAMIN: What things?

(*They laugh.*)

BARBARA: One morning—always in the morning—you started talking about Mom.

RICHARD: Mom?

BARBARA: (*To* BENJAMIN) You said you once bought her a coat. Remember? (*To* JANE) It might be the one I still have. The purple one, from the fifties?

JANE: That we kept in the dress-up trunk?

BARBARA: That one.

(JANE *turns to* RICHARD.)

JANE: The one your dog chewed half up, Richard.

RICHARD: It wasn't my dog.

BARBARA: You brought him here.

RICHARD: How did I know he was sick—?

(TIM *enters with a sweater and a suitcase.*)

TIM: I brought in our suitcase. Where do I put this?

BARBARA: You're in the living room. Marian's getting you sheets and towels…

JANE: *(About the sweater to* BARBARA*)* Tim's daughter gave me this for my birthday, Barbara.

TIM: I paid for it.

JANE: *(To* JANE*)* You said, she picked it out.

BARBARA: It's lovely. You have to bring your daughter—

TIM: Karen.

BARBARA: Karen. Up to Rhinebeck sometime.

TIM: I'll ask her. *(He goes off.)*

BARBARA: Tim has a daughter??

JANE: She's nine.

(Off from the living room, the Kyrie *from Durufle's* Requiem, *as heard at the beginning of the play, begins to play.)*

BARBARA: *(She hears the music)* What is she doing? Marian?

JANE: What?

RICHARD: She was playing that when I arrived. I told you. It's from your Christmas concert.

BARBARA: Yes.

RICHARD: *(To* JANE*)* Barbara's community chorus. A C D of one of their concerts last year.

*(*TIM *returns.)*

BARBARA: Tim, did Marian put that music on?

TIM: She was putting it on when I went in. *(To* JANE*)* What should I do now?

JANE: We're just picking up… Just clean up…

BARBARA: *(Listening)* I hadn't known what the word 'requiem' meant, until we sang this. It means 'Rest.'

TIM: *(To* RICHARD*)* I've sung this.

*(*BARBARA *listens.)*

BARBARA: Evan is in—. Evan was in our chorus… She's singing in this. She's on that…

(This stops everyone.)

BARBARA: Marian would never let me play it…

JANE: Evan?

BARBARA: Evan was an alto too. She usually was in the row in front of me… *(Listening. To* BENJAMIN *who is listening)* Remember this, Uncle? Remember Evan?

BENJAMIN: Evan?

*(*MARIAN *comes out.)*

MARIAN: We should go.

JANE: *(To* MARIAN*)* We're picking up.

(They begin to pick up.)

RICHARD: We want to get good seats.

(As the music plays they take up the table cloth, pile plates, clean crumbs.)

MARIAN: *(At the table)* Barbara, there are a few stains. [on the tablecloth]

*(*BARBARA *starts to stand.)*

MARIAN: I'll do it. *(She begins to fold up the tablecloth.)*

*(*JANE *stops on her way out to the kitchen:)*

JANE: *(To* MARIAN*)* Evan is singing on this?

*(*MARIAN *looks to* BARBARA, *then:)*

MARIAN: She is.

(JANE *goes,* MARIAN *folds up the tablecloth.* BARBARA *takes dishes off.* JANE *returns.)*

JANE: Let's go, Uncle. We need to go now...

(JANE *goes off with* BENJAMIN—*they are all aware that they are letting* MARIAN *listen to her daughter.)*

(*As* BARBARA *folds up the card table, she is stopped by:)*

MARIAN: *(Pointing out a moment in the music)* The altos...

(RICHARD *has returned and takes the card table. He and* BARBARA *go off, and for a moment* MARIAN *is left alone.)*

(MARIAN *tries not to cry.)*

MARIAN: *(To the music, to her daughter)* Bye...

(*And* MARIAN *follows the others and goes off. The music ends.)*

END OF PLAY

NOTE

SWEET AND SAD is the second in a series of plays about The Apple Family, set in Rhinebeck, New York; where I live. The first was THAT HOPEY CHANGEY THING which opened at the Public Theater on election night, November 2, 2010, the night it was set. Each of the following plays will follow this principle and will be written to open on the day they are set.

In a note for HOPEY CHANGEY, I wrote that because these plays are "so completely tied to very specific times, [their] references and even concerns are certain to be soon out of date." And so, hence, they might be called "disposable" plays. And I said, I accepted that.

Since then, I have begun to hedge a little on this; and have wondered or fantasized that after the (imagined) four plays of this series are completed, that there might be something in putting them all together into one very long evening; the hope being that the very specificity of the plays combined with the over-riding arc of them covering the same people over several years, might tell a rich and compelling story. So instead of feeling dated, the plays, as a whole, might just feel true. We'll see. As I say, it might all be a fantasy.

But what I do know is that writing these plays, which are so incredibly specific in time and place, has been liberating for this writer. I feel I have found a way to address my questions of our society/culture/time/ politics that derives not from ideas or (God help us) an ideology, but rather from human beings talking to human beings.

I wrote in the earlier note: "We have become used to viewing our politics and our political landscape through the lens of journalists or commentators or, now, comedians. Their observations are certainly invaluable to us and the very best of them struggle valiantly to be a check on vanity, arrogance, ignorance and stupidity. However, what has been missing from our political forum is the individual's voice." And so I write it again, as this is as appropriate, I hope, for SWEET AND SAD as it was for HOPEY CHANGEY.

The theater has a unique place in the history of societies. After all, the theater is the only artistic form that *uses the entire live human being as its expression*; and hence, carries within itself a very specific view of the world; and that view, in a word, is humanistic. The individual is at the center of the play, and the world of the play revolves around the individual—that is simply what a play is. By a play's very nature, the heart of any play is the individual voices of its characters. And in times like our own, when human voices seem more disembodied than ever, where words seem pulled from their meanings and turned into rants and weapons, the theater can, I believe, be a necessary home for human talk; that is, a place where humans beings talk about their worries, confusions, fears and loves. And where they also listen.

So in one sense then, I'm hoping that these plays, both HOPEY CHANGEY and SWEET AND SAD as well as those to come, are plays about the need to talk, the need to listen, and the need for theater.

I read numerous books and articles while writing SWEET AND SAD and some have influenced the play, in large and small ways. In particular, Matt Taibbi's enjoyable *Gritftopia* is the book that Tim has been reading, and that has been depressing him so much. Others: Paul Goldberger's *Up From Zero*, Robert B Reich's *After Shock*, Marian Klamkin's *The Return of Lafayette*. Tim's story about the rescue of Yiddish books comes from a video I saw at the extraordinary Yiddish Book Center in Amherst, Massachusetts, in which the founder describes the beginnings of the Center.

And as I wrote previously, these plays, including SWEET AND SAD, are works of fiction, and not based upon any living person or persons.

R N
Rhinebeck

www.ingramcontent.com/pod-product-compliance
Lightning Source LLC
Chambersburg PA
CBHW052139090426
42741CB00009B/2151